SPIRAL GUIDE

CROATIA

W0008726

AA
Publishing

Contents

Written by Tony Kelly

Designed by Nucleus Design
Copy edited by Karen Pieringer
Verified by Lindsay Bennett
Indexed by Marie Lorimer

Published by AA Publishing, a trading name of Automobile
Association Developments Limited, whose registered office is Fanum
House, Basing View, Basingstoke, Hampshire RG21 4EA.
Registered number 1878835.

ISBN-10: 0-7495-4739-1
ISBN-13: 978-0-7495-4739-4

The contents of this publication are believed correct at the time of
printing. Nevertheless, AA Publishing accept no responsibility for
errors, omissions or changes in the details given, or for the conse-
quences of readers' reliance on this information. This does not
affect your statutory rights. Assessments of the attractions, hotels
and restaurants are based upon the author's own experience and
contain subjective opinions that may not reflect the publisher's
opinion or a reader's experience. We have tried to ensure accuracy,
but things do change, so please let us know if you have any
comments or corrections.

A CIP catalogue record for this book is available from the
British Library.

Cover design and binding style by permission of AA Publishing
Colour separation by Leo Reprographics
Printed and bound in China by Leo Paper Products

Find out more about AA Publishing and the wide range of travel
publications and services the AA provides by visiting our website at
www.theAA.com/travel

A03214
Maps produced from data supplied by Global Mapping, Brackley,
UK. Copyright © Global Mapping/Hibernia

the magazine

1,001 Dalmatians –

Island-hopping in the Adriatic

Picture the scene. You've spent all day relaxing on the deck of your own yacht, sailing past herb-scented islands and stopping to swim in a turquoise cove. Towards dusk, you arrive at a pretty little fishing port and someone throws you a rope from the jetty. You tie up your boat, step ashore and spend the evening at a waterside restaurant, sipping chilled wine and eating fresh fish as the sun slowly goes down.

Facts and Figures

- 1,185 islands, about 50 of which are inhabited
- 5,835km (3,625 miles) of coastline
- 4,058km (2,522 miles) of which is on islands
- 50 marinas
- 350 natural harbours
- 13,000 berths

Above: view across the rooftops of Rovinj from the campanile

With more than 1,000 islands and clear, calm seas, it is no wonder that sailors love the Croatian coast. In recent years, Croatia has emerged as a serious rival to Greece and Turkey as the Mediterranean's top sailing destination.

Island-hopping

There are two main ways of island-hopping in the Adriatic. One is to use the excellent network of ferries, most of them run by Jadrolinija (► 36), who link the ports of Zadar, Split and Dubrovnik to the major inhabited islands. The other is to take your own boat. You can charter yachts locally, or arrange it in advance (see panel). The basic choice is between a bareboat charter, where at least one member of the crew must be an experienced sailor, and a skippered

Left: calm waters off Zlatni Rat beach, near Bol

boat, where you can help with the sailing, but pay extra for a captain in charge. Some operators also offer full-service yachts, complete with a captain, cook, steward and hostess. Another alternative is to join a flotilla, where you have to be able to sail your own boat, but are part of a larger party where expert help is available if required.

In your own yacht, you can choose where to stop, perhaps mooring one night in a chic waterside town and the next in a deserted bay. Most of the 50 marinas are open all year and all are within a day's sailing of each other. For a real back-to-nature experience, head for the uninhabited islands of the Kornati archipelago near Zadar. Just look out for the *bora*, a strong northeasterly wind that blows from the mainland to the sea.

Useful Websites

- www.jadrolinija.hr (ferry routes and timetables)
- www.aci-club.hr (operators of 21 marinas)
- www.ayc.hr (Adriatic Yacht Charter)
- www.charter.com (online charter booking engine)
- www.croatia.hr (full list of marinas and yacht charters)
- www.sailcroatia.net (bareboat and skippered charters)
- www.sailingholidays.com (flotilla holidays)

Just off the courtyard of the Sponza Palace in Dubrovnik is a memorial room to the victims of the 1991–2 siege. To many visitors, the photos of dead teenagers, shattered buildings and the torn remnants of a Croatian flag from the summit of Mount Srđ provide a shocking reminder of the realities of war.

Stay in one of the buzzing coastal resorts in summer and you could be forgiven for forgetting the most important fact about Croatia – that this is a young country, born out of the former Yugoslavia and still recovering from the wars that tore it apart little over a decade ago. Head inland to Vukovar, or the Serb villages around Knin, and the scars of war are there for all to see in the burned-out houses and pockmarked façades. The emotional damage is less visible, but it exists all the same. The few Croats and Serbs who remain in these areas share an uneasy peace, leading separate lives, drinking in separate bars and sending their children to separate schools.

In many ways, Croatia is still in denial about what it calls the Homeland War. There are no national war

5 August, 1995, near the Adriatic coast, shortly before Croatian troops captured the strategic town of Knin from rebel Serbs

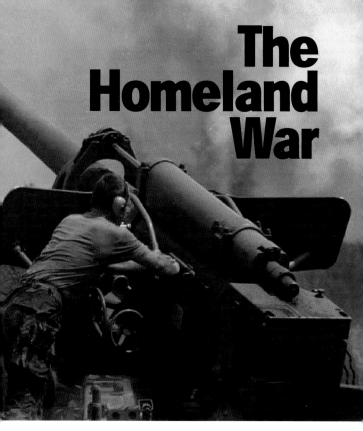

The Homeland War

memorials, unless you count pile of bricks on a Zagreb reet corner, each brick presenting one dead body. he symbols of nationalism re everywhere, though most oliticians prefer to focus on ie future, portraying Croatia s a modern, orward-looking uropean nation. ut the world is ot so easily onvinced. Talks n entry to the uropean Union ere held up in 005 over Croatia's inability unwillingness to track own fugitive generals anted by the international ar crimes tribunal in The lague. Many of the soldiers accused of war crimes are still heroes in Croatia.

"Many of the soldiers accused of war crimes are still heroes in Croatia"

End of an Era

In hindsight, the wars of 1991–5 were an inevitable consequence of the break-up of Yugoslavia. The country had been held together by President Tito (1892–1980), a Croatian Communist fighter who came to power in 1945 after leading the Partisan resistance movement against both the Ustaše puppet régime of Croatia and the royalist Serbian Chetniks during World War II. For 35 years, Tito managed to unite

Never Mind the Balkans

You have to watch your language in Croatia. Most people have traditionally referred to the Yugoslav states as part of the Balkan peninsula, but these days Balkan is a dirty word. Political leaders repeatedly call Croatia a Central European nation, emphasizing its historic links with Austria, Hungary and Italy, and downplaying the Serbian connection. In truth, Croatia stands at the crossroads of cultures as it has done ever since the Roman empire split into eastern and western spheres. Torn for centuries between Venice and Istanbul, Catholic and Orthodox, it is no surprise that Croatia and Serbia were the catalysts for the worst war in Europe since 1945.

the various people of the Balkans – Croats, Serbs, Slovenians, Macedonians, Bosnians, Albanians and 1991 and was attacked by units of the Yugoslav People's Army (JNA), a largely pro-Serb military based in

Evidence of gun damage

others – behind his own brand of socialism, rejecting both Western-style democracy and Soviet-style Communism, and combining the methods of dictatorship with large elements of personal freedom.

Ten years after Tito's death, Yugoslavia fell apart. Croatia declared independence in

Belgrade. On the pretext of protecting the Serbian minority in Croatia, Yugoslav forces started to move into Serb-populated villages, establishing the Republic of the Serbian Krajina at Knin. Before long, the Serbs controlled a third of Croatia, mostly in the border areas of

> **"Ten years after Tito's death, Yugoslavia fell apart."**

Dalmatia and Slavonia, cutting off road and rail links from Zagreb to Split and evicting Croats from their homes in a practice which came to be known as 'ethnic cleansing'. When Operation Storm ended the Serbian occupation in 1995, the situation was reversed as most Serbs fled into Bosnia. Although the war officially ended in 1995, parts of eastern Slavonia, including Vukovar, were not returned to Croatia until 1998.

Croatia's war leader was Franjo Tuđman (1922–99), a former Yugoslav general who became a hard-line Croatian nationalist and the first president of independent Croatia. His successor, Stjepan Mesić, has adopted a much more liberal, pro-Western attitude,

Bronze statue of Tito in Kumrovec

negotiating with the European Union and co-operating with the war crimes tribunal.

In 2005, he was elected to serve a second five-year term. Whether he can finally silence the ghosts of war remains to be seen.

Naturism – The Naked Truth

As the tour boats enter the mouth of the Limski Kanal, the passengers on board take out their cameras and binoculars to admire the view. Some of them get rather more than they were expecting, for this is the site of the biggest naturist colony in Europe.

The tradition of nude sunbathing in Croatia goes back a while. The first official naturist beach opened on Rab in 1934. Two years later, the British king Edward VIII and his lover Wallis Simpson asked permission to swim naked in Kandarola Bay. Croatia has had a laid-back attitude to nudity ever since.

Embracing the Culture

While other countries tolerated nudism and confined it to out-of-the-way places, Croatia wholeheartedly embraced it, opening Europe's first commercial naturist resorts in the 1960s. Koversada, which began in 1961 on a small islet off Vrsar, has grown into a mega-resort, with space for 7,000 people staying in campsites, bungalows and apartments. There are restaurants, shops, children's playgrounds, tennis courts (sports clothing optional), mini-golf, beach volleyball and sailing boats for rent. This is merely the biggest of some 30 official naturist resorts, many of them in Istria.

What is Naturism?

Naturism is defined by the International Naturist Federation as 'a way of living in harmony with nature, characterized by the practice of communal nudity'. It is not to be confused with sex or eroticism – as any visit to a naturist beach will quickly confirm. You can find more information on naturism in Croatia on the Croatia Naturally website at www.cronatur.com

You can dress as nature intended at hundreds of remote beaches and coves on the Adriatic islands and coast. As a general rule, the further you go off the beaten track, the more acceptable nudity becomes. Ask around at any busy harbour in summer and you will find boats willing to take you to FKK (freikörperkultur or 'free body culture') beaches on nearby islands. Even at mainstream beaches, there is usually a section where nudity is tolerated.

The distinction between naturists and 'textiles' (people who wear clothes) in Croatia is gradually breaking down. Around 10 per cent of all visitors to Croatia sunbathe naked at some point, and topless female bathing is the norm. In the past, FKK beaches were strictly for naturists but these days 'clothing optional' is the rule. If you do visit a nudist beach and decide to keep your clothes on, just remember that staring is rude and photography is definitely out. And if you take your clothes off – don't forget the sunblock.

Most Croatian beaches, such as Bol, on Brač, have a secluded corner for naturists

The Best of Croatia

Ten Special Experiences

- A walk around Dubrovnik's city walls (➤ 149)
- The view of Rovinj on the boat trip from Crveni Otok (➤ 98)
- Joining the evening *korzo* to see the beautiful people of Zagreb (➤ 47)
- Walking among lakes and waterfalls in the Plitvička Jezera (➤ 70–72) or Krka (➤ 118–119) national parks
- Sitting on the deck of the early-morning ferry from Split to one of the Adriatic islands
- Sipping Prošek (sweet red wine) on a summer evening by the sea
- Taking in a concert at the Roman amphitheatre in Pula (➤ 112)
- Getting away from it all on a farm in the Zagorje (➤ 86) or Lonjsko Polje (➤ 85)
- Cruising through the uninhabited islands of the Kornati archipelago (➤ 134)
- Taking off your clothes and getting back to nature on one of Croatia's many naturist beaches (➤ 12–13)

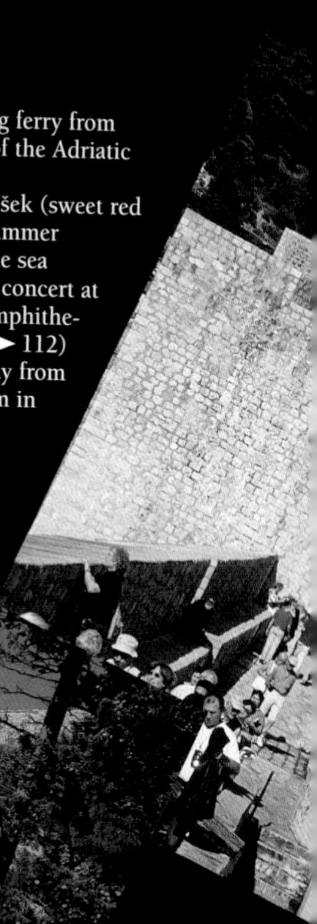

Left: Makarska

Above: Dubrovnik's city walls

Above right: *pršut* (prosciutto), cheese, olives and bread

Five Character Hotels

- Pucić Palace, Dubrovnik (➤ 158)
- Villa Dubrovnik, Dubrovnik (➤ 159)
- Villa Angelo d'Oro, Rovinj (➤ 109)
- Mozart, Opatija (➤ 108)
- Livadić, Samobor (➤ 86)

Ten Things To Try While You're There

- *Pršut*: cured ham from Istria or Dalmatia, similar to an Italian prosciutto
- *Paški sir*: strong sheep's cheese from the island of Pag
- *Čevapčići*: popular snack of grilled meat rissoles, served with raw onions, bread and *ajvar* (aubergine and pepper relish)
- *Crni rižot*: black risotto, coloured with cuttlefish ink
- *Brudet*: Dalmatian fish stew
- *Pasticada*: Dalmatian dish of veal cooked in sweet wine
- Truffles from Istria
- Oysters from Ston
- *Dingač* red wine from the Pelješac peninsula
- *Biska* (mistletoe brandy) from Istria

Best Beaches

One of Croatia's drawbacks is its lack of sandy beaches – most are either rocky, pebbled or man-made concrete sunbathing platforms with steps into the sea. The best-known beach is at Zlatni Rat on Brač (➤ 126–128), a stunning shingle spit backed by pine woods. The beaches along the Makarska Rivijera (➤ 136) offer a mix of sand and pebbles and are suitable for children.

There are good sandy beaches at:
- Baška, on the island of Krk (➤ 106)
- Lopar, on the island of Rab (➤ 106)
- Sabunike, near Nin (➤ 133)
- Lovrečina, on the island of Brač (➤ 128)
- Saplunara, on the island of Mljet (➤ 151)
- Prižna, at Lumbarda on the island of Korčula (➤ 154)
- Šunj, at Lopud on the Elafiti Islands (➤ 156)

Staying on the Farm

Živko Matošević makes wine in the village of Kloštar in Istria. Miroslav Ravlić keeps pigs on the flood plains of the Lonjsko Polje near Zagreb. The two men have never met, but they are both part of a growing movement which is changing the way that tourists see their country.

In the old days, visitors to Croatia stayed in one of the big package hotels on the coast, spending their days on the beaches and their nights in the hotel bar, seeing very little of Croatia beyond their chosen resort. When tourism collapsed as a result of the 1991–5 war, the local people

The rural landscape of Zagorje

ecided to take a fresh look. These days, the buzzwords are 'rural tourism' as more and more people return to their roots and open their houses to a new wave of adventurous visitors.

Agrotourism

Agrotourism is breathing new life into rural Croatia. Old villages which were almost abandoned are being repopulated by a younger generation, eager to restore dilapidated stone farmhouses and develop organic agriculture. Driving through the inland regions, you come across roadside signs advertising *agroturizam, seoski turizam* or *seljački turizam*, which all mean much the same thing. It could be a stone cottage with a couple of spare rooms, or a grand farmhouse that has been turned into a luxury rural hotel, complete with a swimming pool in the grounds.

Istria...

Istria is where agrotourism is at its most developed, helped by the local tourist authorities who have set up wine and olive oil routes and bicycle trails to encourage visitors inland. A booklet of farmstays, available at tourist offices, is published each year and the website lists over 200 properties (www.istra.com/agroturizam).

With its olive groves, vineyards and Tuscan-style hill towns, Istria makes the perfect agrotourism destination, especially as the sea is never far away. After an afternoon on the beach, what could be better than to return to your cosy farmhouse for a home-cooked meal of fresh local produce, accompanied by the farmer's own wine and a welcome glass of herb brandy?

...and beyond

Other areas where agrotourism is taking off include the Zagorje, north of Zagreb; the villages around the Plitvice Lakes; and the Baranja region of northeast Slavonia, near the Kopački Rit wetlands. You will also find examples of rural tourism on some of the larger islands, such as Korčula and Hvar. Some places offer horse-riding and bicycles for rent; others will let you join in with everything from feeding the animals to picking grapes and searching for wild mushrooms. Facilities vary, but what they all share is the chance for an insight into rural life.

A village church in Zagorje

Lighthouses

If you really want to get away from it all, you could stay in a lighthouse on the Adriatic coast. Eleven of them have been converted into apartments, sleeping between two and eight people. All apartments have electricity or gas, hot and cold water, TV and a kitchen, though you will have to take your own provisions for the week. Three of the lighthouses – at Makarska, Poreč and Savudrija – are on the mainland close to restaurants and shops; the one at Savudrija, on Istria's northern tip, is the oldest in Croatia, built in 1818. The others are all on islands, with varying degrees of isolation. The lighthouse at Palagruža, built in 1875, stands 90m (295 feet) above the sea on the remotest island in the Adriatic, 70km (43 miles) from Vis and halfway between the Croatian and Italian coasts. The island is 1,400m (4,590 feet) long and 300m (985 feet) wide, with its own beach and excellent fishing. Boat transfers can be arranged from Korčula or Split, but once there you are on your own. A VHF radio is on hand to summon a boat or helicopter to the island in an emergency. There are two four-person apartments, and a resident lighthouse keeper for company. Just hope that you all get on with each other. Lighthouse accommodation can be booked through www.adriatica.net or www.lighthouses-penul.com

ARCHITECTURE

Croatia's diversity of architecture is a result of its history and has been a number of influences, ranging from Venice to Vienna.

Roman

The Romans conquered the Adriatic coastline in the 1st century BC, establishing their province of Dalmatia and building cities at Pula and Zadar. The emperor Diocletian was born in the Dalmatian city of Salona in AD 245 and later built his retirement palace at Split.

Highlights
• The arena at Pula (➤ 101)
• The Temple at Pula (➤ 102)
• Diocletian's Palace (➤ 123)

Byzantine

After the Romans, Croatia were ruled by the Byzantine empire and Christianity became the main religion. The Slavic tribes from Ukraine adopted Christianity and built churches influenced by Greek, Latin and Celtic architecture.

Highlights
• The mosaics in the Basilica of Euphrasius at Poreč (➤ 94–95)

Typically neo-classical architecture in Opatija

- The Church of St Donat at Zadar (▶ 133)
- The Church of the Holy Cross at Nin (▶ 133)

Venetian

The finest buildings on the Dalmatian coast were constructed during Venetian rule between the 14th and 18th centuries. Master architects such as Juraj Dalmatinac (George the Dalmatian; c1400–73) and Nikola Firentinac (Nicholas of Florence) employed a transitional style which has come

though in other respects the architecture is similar. Much of Dubrovnik was destroyed in an earthquake in 1667; the uniformity of the city today is due to the fact that it was all rebuilt at the same time.

Highlights
- Šibenik Cathedral (▶ 134)
- Trogir Cathedral (▶ 121)
- The arsenal and theatre at Hvar (▶ 129–132)

Baroque

The extravagant baroque style, characterized by its

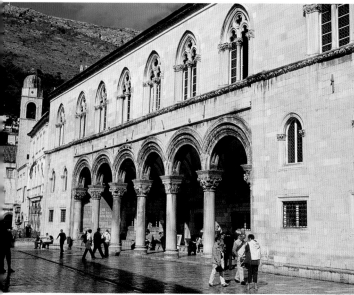

to be known as Gothic-Renaissance. The Sponza Palace and Rector's Palace in Dubrovnik both symbolize this style.

Most towns along the coast have Venetian-style loggias, usually adorned with the winged lion of St Mark, symbol of Venice. Dubrovnik broke free from Venice in 1358, becoming the city-state of Ragusa, so the winged lion is conspicuously absent,

ornate, brightly coloured façades, was popular in northern Croatia during the 18th century as a symbol of Catholicism on the borders of the Ottoman empire. It reached its peak in the town of Varaždin, which was briefly Croatia's capital.

Highlights
- The town centre at Varaždin (▶ 76–77)
- The Tvrđa at Osijek (▶ 83)

Top left: Rom remains at P
Above: the Venetian Rector's Pala at Dubrovnik
Top right: the Byzantine Church of St Donat, Zadar
Above right: baroque interior of Varaždin cathedral

• The Eltz Palace at Vukovar
(► 83)

The 19th-century

The end of the Habsburg era
was marked by grandiose
public buildings combining
elements of classical, Gothic,
Renaissance and baroque
styles. The best examples
can be seen in Zagreb's
Donji Grad.

Highlights
• Trg Bana Jelačića, Zagreb
(► 46–48)
• Croatian National Theatre,
Zagreb (► 64)
• The seafront villas and
promenade at Opatija
(► 104)

Dubrovnik's walls

The restoration of Dubrovnik's city walls is one of the great success stories of
modern Croatia. During the siege of 1991–2, they were repeatedly shelled and
some of the citizens took refuge in the fortresses. Today, tourists once again stroll
around the ramparts of this World Heritage city and there are few visible signs of
damage. The walls date from the 15th century, at a time when the republic of
Ragusa felt itself under threat from the growing Ottoman empire, following the fall
of Constantinople in 1453. The main towers were the work of Michelozzo
Michelozzi (1396–1472), chief architect to the Medici family of Florence; among
others who worked on the walls was Juraj Dalmatinac, architect of Šibenik cathedral. Up to 25m (82 feet) high in places, and supported by two free-standing
fortresses outside the Pile and Ploče gates, the walls were not breached until
Napoleon's troops entered the city in 1806. Ironically, the attack on the walls in
1991 first drew international attention to the war in Croatia; after the war, money
poured in for their restoration

Wild Croatia – River Deep, Mountain High

Mountains, lakes, rivers, waterfalls, forests, canyons and a sparkling blue sea – if you want spectacular natural scenery, Croatia has it all.

About 40 per cent of the country is mountainous, with the rugged peaks and grey karst limestone of the Dinaric range providing a natural border with Bosnia and a dramatic backdrop to the Adriatic coast. The highest peak is Mount Dinara (1,831m/6,007 feet) near Knin. Carved through by gorges and riddled with underground rivers and caves, the Dinaric Mountains extend out to sea, their

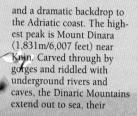

partially submerged summits forming the barren islands of Pag and the Kornati archipelago. Another 30 per cent of Croatia is covered in forests of oak, pine, fir, beech and spruce.

Croatia has always been passionate about preserving its natural heritage. The first national park was established in 1949 at the Plitvice Lakes. There are now eight national parks where wildlife is protected and tourism carefully controlled (see panel). A further ten nature parks include the Kopački Rit (► 78–79) and Lonjsko Polje (► 80–81) flood plains and Mount Medvednica (► 59) north of Zagreb. Nature parks offer a slightly lower level of protection and access is generally free to visitors, whereas there is a fee to enter the national parks.

Wildlife

• As well as bears (see panel below), other large mammals which thrive in Croatia's mountains and forests include lynx, wolf and wild boar, all of which may be seen in the Plitvice Lakes, North Velebit and Risnjak national parks. Red and roe deer are also common, and mouflon, a wild mountain sheep, are found on the Biokovo massif, behind Makarska.

Main picture: reed beds around Vransko Jezero

Inset: the elusive brown bear

The Bear Facts

It is estimated that between 400 and 600 European brown bears live in the Gorski Kotar and Velebit mountain ranges, including the Plitvice Lakes and Risnjak national parks. The brown bear is the largest living land carnivore, weighing up to 300kg (660 pounds), but typically averaging between 100 and 150kg (220 and 330 pounds). It is highly unlikely that you will see one, as they are generally shy creatures, coming down to the lower slopes at night only to hunt for food. Although most bears hibernate for around three months each winter, it may be possible to see their tracks in the snow. Despite being virtually extinct in other parts of Europe, bears can be legally hunted in Croatia outside the national parks and you may be surprised to find smoked bear meat and pâté on sale in smart restaurants and shops.

Another common mammal is the pine marten, a weasel-like creature which feeds on small rodents and birds. The pine marten has even given its name (*kuna*) to the Croatian currency.

- Birds of prey include golden eagles and peregrine falcons, particularly in the Paklenica and North Velebit mountain ranges, and a colony of griffon vultures on the island of Cres. White and black storks nest in the wetlands of northern Croatia in spring and summer, particularly in the Lonjsko Polje, where you may also see egrets herons and cormorants.
- Common dolphins frequently swim off the Adriatic coast, and there is a school of around 200 bottle-nosed dolphins around the islands of Cres and Lošinj.

The Great Outdoors

Croatia is a paradise for walkers, mountaineers, cyclists, canoeists, sailors, divers, extreme sports enthusiasts and anyone who appreciates the great outdoors. The tradition of mountaineering goes back a long way and the highland regions have an excellent network of well-marked paths and mountain huts. The lower slopes and forests are fine for gentle hiking, but the higher mountains are for serious climbers only. Even in summer, when the coast is bathed in sunshine, there can be snow in the mountains. In winter, the mountain regions are bitterly cold, with sub-zero temperatures the norm. Anyone planning serious

alpine walking should get hold of *Walking in Croatia* by Rudolf Abraham, published by Cicerone Press. For gentler walks, head for the Medvednica range north of Zagreb or the green hills of the Žumberak-Samoborsko Gorje, between Samobor and the Slovenian border.

Rock-climbers could try the challenging faces of the Paklenica and North Velebit national parks. Paklenica, set

Left: the Paklenica National Park offers diverse routes and climbs

Above: a bottle-nosed dolphin

around a pair of parallel limestone gorges plunging down from the Velebit massif to the sea, has more than 400 climbing routes for all levels of ability, including a steep rock wall at the entrance to the gorge which is used by beginners. Alpine and free climbing is also possible on the islands of Brač, Mljet and Vis, and in Zlatni Rat forest park at Rovinj.

Canoeing, kayaking and white-water rafting are all popular activities, with local companies offering numerous excursions on the rivers Kupa, Dobra, Zrmanja and Cetina. Another good choice is the River Una, on the border of Bosnia and Croatia, where the rafting reaches grades 4 and 5.

The top rafting destination is Omiš, at the mouth of the River Cetina, convenient for people staying on the Makarska Rivijera or the central Dalmatian islands.

Just so you know you've arrived

You may see golden eagles in flight, but you are unlikely to get an up-close sighting

National Parks

Sword Dancers o

Leave me alone! Your demands are in vain
My charms belong to another man.

So begins the story of the *moreška* , a ritualized sword dance that arrived on the island of Korčula in the 16th century. The roots of the dance are lost in the mists of time, but its name derives from the Spanish or Italian word for 'Moorish' and it is a variation of the mock battles between Muslim and Christian soldiers which have been performed across the Mediterranean since the time of the Crusades. In Korčula, it was easily adapted to fit the local situation, at a time when the Venetian rulers of Dalmatia faced a constant

threat from the Turkish Ottoman empire to the east.

The story is a familiar tale of good and evil, and as always the good guys come out on top. It opens with the Black King, dressed in black, dragging a pretty Muslim maiden across the stage in chains as he attempts to persuade her to return his unrequited love. The woman, Bula, rejects him because of her love for Osman, the White King, who is confusingly dressed in red.

Eventually the two kings bring on their armies of followers, also dressed in black and red, and the dance begins. To the accompaniment of a brass band, the two armies join battle, forming a

Korčula

circle as they act out the seven different movements of a highly stylized war dance, thrusting and clashing their swords in pairs. Each of the movements has its own rhythm; during the final movement, the sword clashes are fast and furious and sparks fly through the air as the Black King's army retreats into the middle of an ever smaller circle before collapsing, dying and defeated. onto the ground. The Black King surrenders his sword and the White King frees Bula from her chains with a kiss as the audience bursts into applause.

By the end of World War II, the *moreška* had almost died out and there were few people on Korčula who remembered the dance. It was revived by the local barber, schoolteacher, policeman and conductor of the town orchestra. These days, the sword dance is once again a regular feature of life on the island and has become a popular tourist spectacle. Throughout July and August, a Festival of Sword Dances takes place across the island, with performances of *moreška* in Korčula town and the similar *kumpanija* dance in Blato, Smokvica and Vela Luka.

On Monday and Thursday evenings in summer, the Sveta Cecilija dance troupe performs the *moreška* on a special stage outside the Kopnena Vrata (Land Gate). Go if you get the chance – though you will probably be thankful that the modern performance lasts 45 minutes only, instead of the traditional two hours.

Opposite and left: performances of *moreška* enliven the streets of Korčula town in summer

Split Personality

Goran Ivanišević – Croatian tennis star

In July 2001, more than 100,000 people lined the waterfront at Split to welcome a returning hero after one of the most improbable sporting success stories of modern times.

Goran Ivanišević was born in Split in 1971, the son of engineers. As a child, he was a keen footballer and cross-country champion, but it soon became clear that he had a talent for tennis. He turned professional at the age of 17, and by 1992 had risen to number two in the world rankings. That same year, he carried the Croatian flag at the Olympic Games in Barcelona.

Tall and good-looking, Ivanišević always attracted publicity; he was equally well known for his powerful serve and his erratic temperament. He once said that when he went on court, he had to face not only his opponent but also the umpire and himself.

Despite his immense talent, he never seemed to achieve his full potential. Three times in the 1990s, he reached the final of the All-England championships at Wimbledon, only to lose every time.

Sporting Heroes

For a country of 4.5 million people, Croatia has enjoyed remarkable sporting success since independence in 1991.

- The men's football team came third in the 1998 World Cup, beating Germany 3–0 before losing in the semi-finals to the hosts and eventual champions France.
- The men's handball team were Olympic champions in 1996 and 2004, and world champions in 2003.
- The men's basketball team won the silver medal at the 1992 Olympics, losing the final to the US 'Dream Team'.
- The skier Janica Kostelić won three gold and one silver medals at the 2002 Winter Olympics, the first person ever to do so.

Chance in a Million

By 2001, he had slipped to 125 in the rankings, but the authorities at Wimbledon decided to award him a 'wild card' for one last attempt at the tournament. Nobody gave him a serious chance, but after cruising through the early rounds, he knocked out the local hero, Tim Henman, in the semi-final. The exciting final, against Australia's Pat Rafter, was a classic, which Ivanišević won 9–7 in the fifth set. 'This is the greatest day of my life; if I never win another match I will die happy,' he said through his tears in front of the crowds on Centre Court.

Fellow Stars

Goran Ivanišević is the only wild-card player ever to win Wimbledon. But he is not the only Croatian tennis star. His compatriot Iva Majoli became the first Croatian Grand Slam champion when she won the French Open in 1997. Buoyed by their successes, a new generation of tennis players is appearing on the scene. At the start of 2005, Croatia had two men and two women ranked in the top 40 in the world.

The new Ivanišević is Mario Ančić, who also comes from Split; she reached the semi-finals at Wimbledon in 2004.

Croatia's **Blazenko Lackovicin** playing in the handball finals against Germany at the 2004 Athens Olympics

Did You Know?

...that the Croatian name for Croatia is Hrvatska?

...that almost 8 million foreign tourists visited Croatia in 2004, with most coming from Germany, Italy, Austria, Slovenia and the Czech Republic?

...that the population of Croatia is 4.5 million, of whom a million live in or around the capital Zagreb? There are also a similar number of Croatians living abroad, including more than a million in the USA and Canada.

...that the tie developed out of a silk scarf, worn by Croatian officers during the Thirty Years War of 1618–48? The style was copied by French dandies at the court of Louis XIV and became known as dressing *à la croate* – the origin of the modern word 'cravat'.

...that the White House in Washington DC was built with stone from the Adriatic island of Brač?

...that the Hollywood stars Sharon Stone and John Malkovich both have homes on the Dalmatian coast?

...that the renowned traveller and explorer Marco Polo (1254–1324) is believed to have been born on the island of Korčula?

...that the unit of magnetic induction is named after the Croatian engineer Nikola Tesla (1856–1943)?

...that the spotted dogs known as Dalmatians are named after a region of Croatia, even though there is little evidence of them having originated there?

...that the Croatian Slavoljub Penkala (1871–1922) is credited with inventing the world's first mechanical pencil and fountain pen?

Finding Your Feet

First Two Hours

Arriving by Air

Croatia's main international airport is at Zagreb, with regular flights on Croatia Airlines to all major European capitals. In summer, most visitors fly directly to one of the coastal airports at Dubrovnik, Split, Zadar, Rijeka and Pula.

Zagreb
• Zagreb airport is at **Pleso**, 17km (10.5 miles) south of the city.
• **Facilities in the arrivals hall** include a bank, ATMs (cash machines), post office and car-rental agencies.
• Croatia Airlines **shuttle buses** run once or twice an hour to a terminal beside the bus station in Zagreb. The journey takes 30 minutes and ticket (25kn) can be bought on the bus. From the bus station, it is a 20-minute walk to central Zagreb or tram No. 6 runs directly to the main square, Trg Bana Jelačića.
• A **taxi to central Zagreb** from outside the arrivals hall will cost around 150kn to 200kn.

Dubrovnik
• Dubrovnik airport is at **Čilipi**, 20km (12 miles) south of the city near Cavtat.
• **Facilities in the arrivals hall** include a bank, ATMs (cash machines), post office and car-rental agencies.
• Croatia Airlines **shuttle buses** drop passengers at the bus station and outside the Pile Gate for access to the old city. The journey takes 30 minutes and tickets (30kn) can be bought on the bus.
• **Taxis cost** around 200kn to central Dubrovnik and 80kn–100kn to Cavtat.

Split
• Split airport is at **Kaštela**, 25km (15.5 miles) north of the city near Trogir
• **Facilities in the arrivals hall** include a bank, ATMs (cash machines), post office and car-rental agencies.
• Croatia Airlines **shuttle buses** drop passengers on the waterfront Riva. The journey takes 30 minutes and tickets (30kn) can be bought on the bus.
• A **taxi to central Split** from costs around 150kn to 200kn.

Airport Information
Zagreb
Tel: 01 456 5222; www.zagreb-airport.hr
Dubrovnik
Tel: 020 773100; www.airport-dubrovnik.hr
Split
Tel: 021 203555; www.split-airport.hr
Zadar
Tel: 023 205800; www.zadar-airport.hr
Rijeka
Tel: 051 842132; www.rijeka-airport.hr
Pula
Tel: 052 530105; www.airport-pula.hr

Arriving by Land

• There are **border crossings** with Slovenia, Hungary, Bosnia-Hercegovina and the republic of Serbia and Montenegro.
• Visitors **arriving from Italy** must pass briefly through Slovenia on their way into Croatia.
• **Citizens of EU countries** entering via Hungary and Slovenia will face minimal formalities at the border.
• If you are **bringing your own car**, you will need to show a driving licence, insurance papers and registration or ownership documents. If you have rented a car in another country, you must get the rental documents stamped to confirm that your insurance is valid in Croatia.
• **Buses from European destinations** arrive at the main bus station in Zagreb. Central Zagreb is a 20-minute walk or a short ride on tram No. 6.
• **Trains from Venice, Vienna, Budapest** and other destinations arrive at the railway station in Zagreb. Central Zagreb is a 10-minute walk away or a short ride on tram No. 6 or 13.

Arriving by Sea

Car and passenger ferries from Italy arrive at the ports of Zadar, Split and Dubrovnik. In summer, there are extra services to the more popular islands and also to Pula and Rovinj in Istria. All of these ports are within walking distance of the city centre, except Dubrovnik. From Gruž harbour in Dubrovnik, buses 1A and 1B run to the main bus station and Pile Gate.

Tourist Information Offices

There are tourist offices in all the main towns, cities and coastal resorts. Most staff speak good English and German and can supply you with free local maps and information. You will also find private tourist agencies operating in most towns and these are usually the best places to find private accommodation and book local excursions. The biggest agency is Atlas (www.atlas-croatia.com), which has offices all over the country. The head office is in Dubrovnik (tel: 020 442222).

Zagreb
✚ Trg Bana Jelačića 11   ☎ 01 481 4051; www.zagreb-touristinfo.hr
Dubrovnik
✚ Stradun   ☎ 020 321561; www.tzdubrovnik.hr
Split
✚ Peristil   ☎ 021 345606; www.visitsplit.com
Pula
✚ Forum 3   ☎ 052 212987; www.pulainfo.hr

Highly populated areas and major routes are now clear of mines and are safe to visit. However, in some isolated areas in the mountains and countryside land mines may still be a danger. You should therefore be careful not to stray from roads and paved areas without an experienced guide.

Admission Charges

The cost of admission for museums and places of interest featured in this guide is indicated by the following price categories.

Inexpensive = under 10kn
Moderate = 10kn–20kn
Expensive = over 20kn

Getting Around

Driving in Croatia

- Drivers **bringing their own cars** into Croatia will need to show a driving licence, insurance certificate and registration documents.
- **Car rental** is available at airports and in all the main towns and resorts. You must be over 21 and have a passport, driving licence and credit card.
- The **best deals** are usually found in advance by booking online through one of the major international chains (see below). If you need a car for a few days only, local companies offer competitive rates, though you should check carefully the levels of insurance cover and excess.
- Keep your passport, driving licence and car rental documents **with you at all times**, and never leave them unattended in the car.

Car Rental Agencies

Budget: tel: 01 480 5688; www.budget.hr
Europcar: tel: 021 604300; www.europcar.com
Hertz: tel: 01 484 6777; www.hertz.hr
Holiday Autos: www.holidayautos.com
National: tel: 021 399043; www.nationalcar.hr
Sixt: 01 655 1599; www.sixt.hr

Driving Essentials

- Drive on the right.
- **Seat belts** are compulsory for the driver and all passengers.
- **Children under 12** must sit in the back of the car.
- The use of **mobile phones** while driving is forbidden.
- **Headlights** must be on at all times.
- **Speed limits** are 50kph (31mph) in urban areas, 90kph (56mph) on minor roads, 110kph (68mph) on main roads and 130kph (80mph) on toll motorways. The maximum speed for vehicles towing caravans is 80kph (50mph).
- A strict **drink-driving law** introduced in 2004 has reduced the blood-alcohol limit to zero. It is now illegal to drive after even moderate consumption of alcohol.
- In the case of an **accident**, you must call the police on 92.
- **Breakdown assistance** is available from Hrvatski Autoklub by calling 987.

Roads and Tolls

- The **A1 motorway** from Zagreb to Split will be extended to Dubrovnik by 2008, cutting several hours off journey times. The distance from Zagreb to Split is 380km (236 miles).
- The **A3 motorway** runs west from Zagreb to the Slovenian border and east to Lipovac on the border with Serbia. This is the Croatian section of the autocesta, the major route across the former Yugoslavia, linking the capitals of Slovenia, Croatia and Serbia.
- **Other motorways** connect Zagreb with Rijeka, Krapina and Goričan on the Hungarian border. Among the roads under construction is a Y-shaped network of motorways throughout Istria, linking Rijeka with Pazin, Pula and Slovenia and eventually joining up with the Italian motorway system.
- All motorways are **subject to tolls**. In most cases you collect a ticket when you enter and pay on exit. Payment can be made in Croatian kuna, euros or by credit card. Typical toll fees for a standard car are 23kn from Zagreb to Varaždin, 56kn from Zagreb to Rijeka and 150kn from Zagreb to Split.

• **Tolls are also charged** for the Učka tunnel linking Rijeka to Istria and the road bridge to Krk.
• The most **scenic drive** in Croatia is the Magistrala highway, which follows the coastline for 600km (372 miles) from Rijeka to Dubrovnik. Although this is a spectacular drive, the road is single-carriageway for most of its length and gets clogged up with holiday traffic in summer.

> Driving Through Bosnia
> Check your insurance carefully if you plan to take a rental car into neighbouring countries, particularly Bosnia-Hercegovina and the republic of Serbia and Montenegro. An exception can be made for the area around Neum, a 9km (5.5-mile) corridor of Bosnia-Hercegovina on the Magistrala highway between Split and Dubrovnik.

Buses and Trains
• **Buses connect the main towns and cities** with outlying villages and coastal resorts.
• **Services range from** luxury air-conditioned inter-city coaches to local buses on the Adriatic islands.
• **Bus fares from the mainland** to the islands, such as Dubrovnik to Korčula or Rijeka to Rab, usually include the cost of the ferry.
• For **timetables and bookings**, ask at the nearest bus station.
• The **railway network** covers most major cities, with the exception of Dubrovnik.
• **Most rail lines** are concentrated in the north and east of the country, making this an efficient way to get around inland Croatia but less useful on the coast.
• **Ultra-modern trains** will soon make the journey from Zagreb to Split in under five hours.
• **For detailed timetables**, contact the main railway station in Zagreb (tel: 060 333444) or see the Croatian Railways website (www.hznet.hr).

City Transport in Zagreb
• Zagreb has an **efficient network** of local buses and trams operated by ZET (www.zet.hr).
• The **main tram hubs** are the railway station, bus station and Trg Bana Jelačića.
• **Maps** are displayed at all tram stops.
• **Tickets** (6.5kn) can be bought from ZET kiosks near the terminals and news kiosks in Trg Bana Jelačića. They are slightly more expensive (8kn) if bought from the driver.
• **Tickets are validated** by punching them in the machine behind the driver.
• There are heavy fines for travelling without a ticket.
• If you are spending a few days in Zagreb, it is worth getting hold of a Zagreb Card, valid for 72 hours. It gives free access to all public transport, including the funicular to Gradec and the Medvednica cable-car, as well as discounts at museums.

City Transport in Dubrovnik
• Buses in Dubrovnik are **operated by Libertas** (www.libertasdubrovnik.hr).
• The **most useful routes** are those connecting the hotels on the Lapad peninsula with the old town.
• Tickets (8kn) can be bought from **news kiosks and Libertas counters** outside the Pile Gate. They are slightly more expensive if bought from the

drivers, who do not give change, so you must pay the exact fare, 10kn.
• Tickets are **validated by punching them** in the machine behind the driver.

Taxis

• Taxis are available in **all main towns**, cities and resorts.
• **Fares are metered**; you usually pay a flat fare of around 25kn plus an extra amount per km, with extra charges levied at night and on Sundays.

Ferries

• The **Jadrolinija ferry company** operates car and passenger services between the mainland and the major islands.
• There is also a **daily car ferry** from Rijeka to Dubrovnik, calling at Zadar, Split, Stari Grad (Hvar), Korčula and Mljet.
• **A full list of routes, fares and timetables** is available from Jadrolinija offices and on the website (www.jadrolinija.hr).
• **Foot passengers** can simply arrive at the harbour and buy tickets from the quayside kiosk.
• **Car passengers** must join a queue, which is often lengthy in summer, so it is best to arrive at least two hours before departure at peak times.
• **Prior reservations** are not possible on local ferries.
• Tickets and cabins for the **main Rijeka to Dubrovnik coastal route** can be booked in advance.
• Between June and September, there are **additional fast catamaran services** linking the islands to the mainland.
• **Catamarans** run throughout the year to the islands of Mljet, Korčula, Hvar, Vis and Lastovo; these are quicker than conventional ferries, but also more expensive and the disadvantage is that you cannot go on deck. Cars are not allowed on these services.
• The timetable is often geared to getting the **islanders to the mainland** for work, so there may only be one boat per day in each direction.

Jadrolinija Offices
Dubrovnik
Tel: 020 418000
Split
Tel: 021 338333
Rijeka
Tel: 051 211444

Accommodation

Croatia has a range of accommodation to suit all budgets and tastes, from large seaside hotels to rooms in private houses. Most hotel rooms in summer are pre-booked by tour operators and package-tourists, but it is almost always possible to find private accommodation by asking around in local agencies or looking for signs advertising *sobe* (rooms) to rent.

Hotels

• The majority of hotels were built during the tourist boom between the 1960s and 1980s. These tend to be **large, modern and well equipped**, though lacking in atmosphere and architectural style. Many have been upgraded since the 1991–95 war, when they were converted to house refugees. Most have swimming pools and a wide range of sports and leisure facilities, restaurants and nightclubs.
• A recent trend has been the opening of **small, family-run and boutique**

hotels in the middle of historic towns. Some of the best examples are listed at the end of the regional chapters.

• **Most hotels on the coast and islands** operate from April to October, while hotels in Zagreb and inland are open all year. Book ahead during the peak months of June, July and August.

• You can search for hotels by region, town and island on **www.croatia.hr**

Private Accommodation

• The **cheapest rooms on the islands and coast** are often in private accommodation. These range from comfortable apartments with kitchen, bathroom and balcony to a spare bedroom with shared bathroom in a family home.

• In **busy tourist towns**, you will be met at the bus station or ferry port by landladies offering rooms or holding up signs saying *sobe* (rooms) or *apartmani* (apartments).

• You can **reserve private rooms** through one of the travel agencies found in all main towns and resorts. This will usually work out a little more expensive, but the accommodation is registered and of a guaranteed standard.

• There are **surcharges for tourist tax** and for stays of less than three days.

Agrotourism

• One of the biggest growth areas has been in **rural farmstays** or agrotourism (► 16–18), which has taken off particularly in Istria and inland areas such as the Zagorje.

• **Rural accommodation** is usually indicated by signs advertising *agroturizam* or *seoski turizam*.

Camping

• Croatia has **over 150 official campsites**, equipped with hot water, showers and toilets. Many have restaurants and sports facilities, including swimming pools.

• The majority are on the coast and islands, while a few are inland beside rivers and lakes. Some of these campsites are **reserved for naturists**.

• Most campsites are **open from May to September**.

• **A full list of campsites** is found at www.croatia.hr and www.camping.hr

Off The Beaten Track

• A number of **lighthouses** have been converted into unusual self-catering accommodation (► 18).

• **Travel agencies in Murter** rent out old stone cottages on the Kornati islands for a 'Robinson Crusoe' experience. There is no electricity or running water; cooking is by gas, water comes from a well and supplies are delivered by boat twice a week. Contact Coronata (tel: 022 435933; www.coronata.hr) or Kornatturist (tel: 022 435854; www.kornatturist.hr).

Accommodation Prices

The symbols refer to the approximate cost per person per night of a double room in summer. Prices drop considerably outside the peak season. Half-board accommodation, which is included in the price of most package holidays, is often only marginally more expensive than bed-and-breakfast. Hotels also levy a tourist tax, which varies according to season.

€ = under 250kn €€ = 250kn–500kn €€€ = over 500kn

Food and Drink

Croatian cuisine is a fascinating blend of Mediterranean, Balkan and Central European influences. Regional cuisines reflect the country's history and geography, with light, fresh, Italian-style cooking dominating on the coast and heavier, spicier fare served in the inland and highland regions.

Eating Out – A Practical Guide

- Most restaurants serve both **Croatian and international dishes**.
- A *konoba* or *gostionica* is a **rustic-style tavern** specializing in more authentic Croatian cuisine.
- **Mealtimes are around** noon–3 for lunch and 7–10 for supper, though most places stay open throughout the day from 9am–11pm.
- Reservations are rarely necessary, except at the **smartest establishments**.
- Most places make a **small cover charge** for bread.
- It is customary to **leave a tip** of around 10 per cent.

What To Eat

- **Starters** include *pršut* (cured ham) and *sir* (cheese).
- **Pasta dishes and risottos** are listed as 'warm starters', but are usually enough for a main course.
- **Fresh fish and seafood** predominate on the coast. Fish (*riba*) is usually plain grilled and sold by weight. Other popular dishes are seafood risotto, octopus salad, shrimps *buzara* (with garlic and white wine) and *brudet* (Dalmatian fish stew).
- **Dalmatian meat dishes** include *pastičada* (beef stewed with sweet wine), *janjetina* (spit-roast lamb) and veal or lamb cooked under a *peka* (metal bell) placed in the embers of a fire.
- **Istrian cooking** is heavily influenced by Italy, featuring *njoki* (gnocchi), *fuži* (pasta) and truffles.
- **Steaks and schnitzels** are popular everywhere, but especially in the inland regions. In Zagreb, look out for *zagrebački odrezak*, a breaded schnitzel stuffed with ham and cheese.
- **Inland and mountain cuisine** is similar to that of central Europe, with dishes such as *gulaš* (goulash) and *grah* (bean stew).
- Slavonian cooking is particularly spicy, featuring *kulen* (salami) and *fiš paprikaš* (fish stew).
- The **national snack** is *ćevapčići*, grilled meatballs served with raw onions, *ajvar* (spicy aubergine and pepper relish) and bread or chips.
- **Side dishes** include chips, boiled potatoes, rice, pasta, salads and *blitva*, which is similar to spinach and is either steamed or fried with potatoes, garlic and olive oil.
- *Pekarnica* (bakeries) sell a wide range of **breads**, as well as *burek* (filo pastry stuffed with minced meat or cheese).
- **Desserts** include *palačinke* (pancakes) with walnuts, chocolate or jam. A *slastičarnica* is a pastry-shop; most also sell delicious ice-cream.

What To Drink

- Croatia produces an **excellent variety of wines**. Cheaper local wines are sold by the litre, whereas more expensive wines are sold by the bottle.
- **Red wines** to look out for include Dingač, Postup and Plavac Mali from the Pelješac peninsula, and Teran from Istria.
- **White wines** include Malvazija from Istria, Graševina from Slavonia, Grk and Pošip from Korčula and Vugava from Vis.

- Prošek is a **sweet red wine** from Dalmatia, drunk as an apéritif or dessert wine.
- **Mixed drinks** include *bevanda* (wine and water), *gemišt* (white wine spritzer), *bambus* (red wine and cola) and *miš-maš* (red wine and Fanta).
- The best brands of **lager** are Karlovačko and Ožujsko. Tomislav is a dark beer from Zagreb.
- Fierce **grappa-like spirits** are drunk both before and after the meal, and are sometimes offered on the house by waiters. They include *šljivovica* (plum brandy), *travarica* (herb brandy) and *biska* (mistletoe brandy from Istria). A sweeter alternative is *orahovac* (walnut liqueur).
- *Mineralna voda* (mineral water) can be either *gazirana* (sparkling) or *negazirana* (still).
- Bars sell **fruit juices**, as well as international brands of soft drinks.
- **Coffee** is usually espresso or cappuccino, though some restaurants serve Turkish coffee, traditionally drunk at home by Croatians.

Food Prices
Approximate prices for a starter, main course, salad and house wine or water.
€ = under 100kn €€ = 100kn–150kn €€€ = over 150kn

Shopping

Croatia has come a long way since the days of state communism, when bland department stores and supermarkets were notable mainly for their empty shelves. Consumerism is no longer a dirt word and the big cities have boutiques and fashion stores to rival neighbouring Italy. Zagreb is the undisputed shopping capital of Croatia, though you will also find a good range of shops in Split, Dubrovnik and elsewhere.

Practicalities
- Most shops are open Monday to Friday from 8 to 8, and Saturday from 9 to 2, although some **close in the middle of the day**, opening from around 9 to 1 and 5 to 8. In larger towns and coastal resorts in season, many stay open on Sundays.
- **Markets** are generally open Monday to Saturday from 8 to 2, though a few open on Sundays as well.
- The monthly **agricultural fairs** in the towns of inland Istria, such as Buzet, Motovun, Pazin and Vodnjan, have traditional local foods, hand-made goods, folk music and dancing. Ask at local tourist offices.
- **Credit cards** are accepted in an increasing number of shops.

What To Buy
- **Popular souvenirs** include lace from Pag, lavender products from Hvar, jewellery from Dubrovnik and gingerbread hearts from around Zagreb.
- **Artists sell their work** in the street at many coastal towns in summer. Some of the best places to buy contemporary art are Rovinj, Grožnjan, Dubrovnik and Hlebine.
- A **Croata silk tie** (➤ 30) makes an unusual present.
- Croatian **wines, spirits, truffles and olive oil** all make good souvenirs.
- Farmers at local markets sell a variety of **home-made spirits and liqueurs** in atttractive bottles.

Entertainment

From top-class music and drama to traditional festivals, sports and outdoor activities, there is always something to do in Croatia. More details can be found from tourist offices and in each of the regional chapters of this book.

Music and Drama

• The top venue is the **Croatian National Theatre** in Zagreb (► 64), home to the National Ballet and National Opera. More than 200 performances of drama, ballet and opera are held here each year between September and July. There are also branches of the Croatian National Theatre in Osijek, Rijeka and Split.

• Almost every town along the coast holds a **cultural festival** in summer, with a series of open-air performances under the name of 'Musical Evenings' or 'Summer Nights'.

• The **big events** are the summer festivals in Dubrovnik (► 162) and Split (► 140), with opera and concerts in the streets of the old town.

• Another spectacular concert venue is the **Roman arena in Pula** (► 112).

Folklore and Festivals

• Croatia has a **rich folk music tradition**, from the *klapa* male voice choirs of Dalmatia to the *kolo* dances and *tamburica* (mandolin) music of Slavonia. Many hotels lay on folklore shows for their guests, but for something more authentic, try the International Folklore Festival in Zagreb in July or the folk festivals at Slavonski Brod and Đakovo (► 88).

• The *moreška* **sword dance** (► 26–27) can be seen on Korčula throughout the summer and at the Festival of Sword Dances in July and August.

• Most towns and villages have their own feast day, when the **patron saint's festival** is marked by religious processions, fireworks and dancing.

• The **pre-Lenten Carnival** is also celebrated across the country; the biggest parades are in Rijeka, Samobor and Lastovo.

Sport and Outdoor Activities

• Croatians are passionate about **soccer** and there is huge rivalry between the two biggest teams, Dinamo Zagreb and Hajduk Split. The season lasts from August to May with a two-month winter break between December and February. Most matches are played at weekends and it is usually possible to get tickets.

• Croatia's **biggest tennis event** is the ATP Croatia Open, held at Umag in late July.

• **Swimming** is popular at beaches along the Adriatic coast. There are few sandy beaches, but many resorts have concrete sunbathing platforms with steps into the sea.

• Walking, bicycling, climbing, horseback-riding, canoeing, kayaking and rafting are all possible in Croatia's mountains and rivers, **together with adventure sports** such as paragliding and canyoning.

• On the coast, numerous operators offer **scuba diving excursions**, while windsurfing is possible at Bol on Brač and Viganj on the Pelješac peninsula. Another option is to charter a yacht to explore the Kornati islands (► 134).

Zagreb

Getting Your Bearings

Zagreb, with around a million inhabitants, one in four of the country's population, is easily Croatia's biggest city. This is the political, economic and cultural heart of the nation, which makes it easy to forget that it has only been a state capital since 1991. For most of its history, Zagreb has lived in

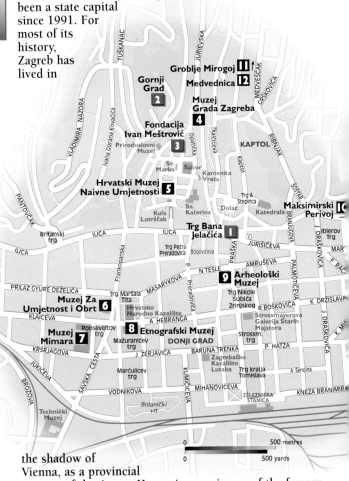

the shadow of Vienna, as a provincial outpost of the Austro-Hungarian empire, or of the former Yugoslav capital Belgrade. Only in the last few years has it rediscovered its confidence as a youthful, vibrant, forward-looking city.

Above: the view of the lake and botanical gardens in Zagreb
Left: Parliament buildings

Zagreb lies between the wooded slopes of Medvednica to the north and the River Sava to the south. It consisted originally of two fortified hilltop settlements – the religious base of Kaptol, still dominated by its cathedral, and the rival political capital of Gradec. Between them, these two make up the area known as Gornji Grad (Upper Town). In the 19th century, the city expanded and the Donji Grad (Lower Town) was developed, with wide boulevards, museums and grand Austro-Hungarian buildings linked by a green 'horseshoe' of parks, promenades and squares. Much of this district was built following an earthquake in 1880, giving the city a unified, central European feel.

The two halves of town meet at Trg Bana Jelačića, Zagreb's central square. With its popular café terraces and hordes of commuters catching trams, the square is busy from morning to night and makes a natural starting point for any visit to the city.

★ Don't Miss

At Your Leisure

This two-day tour makes a perfect introduction for first-time visitors to the city. Spend one day exploring the old town and the other out in the suburbs as you discover the many different faces of Zagreb.

Zagreb in Two Days

Day One

Morning
Start with coffee and pastries on ❶ **Trg Bana Jelačića** (► 46–48), an essential Zagreb experience and the best place to sample the pulse of the city. While you're here, visit the tourist office on the corner of the square to pick up a map and a Zagreb Card (► 48). After coffee, climb the steps to Dolac market (► 63), at its liveliest on weekday mornings.

Lunch
Take the funicular (left) up to ❷ **Gornji Grad** (► 49–51), arriving in time to see the cannon being fired from the Kula Lotrščak (Lotrščak Tower) at noon. Have lunch beneath the tower at Pod Gričkim Topom (► 62), whose terrace offers wonderful views.

Afternoon
Take your time strolling around Gradec, with its churches, palaces and cobbled streets. There are several good museums here, but if you have time for only one, make it the ❸ **Fondacija Ivan Meštrović** (► 52–53), dedicated to the work of Croatia's greatest sculptor. Leave Gradec through the Kamenita Vrata (Stone Gate) and wander back down to Trg Bana Jelačića, pausing to visit the cathedral on the way.

Evening
The streets around Trg Bana Jelačića (right) are at their best during the early evening *korzo*, when people dress up and promenade through the town. Stop for a beer or an ice-cream at one of the outdoor cafés on Bogovićeva before going for dinner at nearby Boban (► 61).

Day Two

Morning

Time to explore Donji Grad (Lower Town). Begin outside the railway station by the equestrian statue of King Tomislav and follow a series of park squares northwards until you reach Trg Nikole Šubića Zrinskog (Zrinjevac), with its bandstand, fountain and statues. On one side of the square is the **9 Archaeological Museum** (➤ 58) – after a quick look around, you can grab a drink at the Lapidarium, a courtyard café surrounded by fragments of Roman sculpture.

Afternoon

Do what the locals do and escape the city for a few hours. The easy option is to hop on tram 11 or 12 from Trg Bana Jelačića for a picnic in **10 Maksimir Park** (➤ 58). Alternatively, take bus No. 106 from outside the cathedral to **11 Mirogoj Cemetery** (➤ 58), then walk down the hill and pick up the tram to **12 Medvednica** (above, ➤ 59). A cable-car whisks you up the mountain; if you have the energy, you can walk back down through the woods before returning to Trg Bana Jelačića by tram.

Evening

Ask at the tourist office for a copy of their monthly leaflet of concert and theatre listings. If you can, take in a show at the Hrvatsko Narodno Kazalište (Croatian National Theatre), a sumptuous opera house which opened in 1895 (➤ 64).

◻ Trg Bana Jelačića

This broad paved square, where the old town meets the new, is the symbolic heart of Zagreb. Café life rules here, with everyone from the president downwards meeting on the café terraces on weekend mornings to read the newspapers, gossip or talk politics and sport. Cars are not allowed in the square, but trams trundle to and fro, bringing commuters and shoppers from the outlying suburbs. With newspaper kiosks and flower stalls against a backdrop of imposing 19th-century Habsburg architecture, Trg Bana Jelačića presents a lively scene.

It was laid out as the city's main square in 1850, but its present character dates from 1866, when the **equestrian statue** of Governor Josip Jelačić (1801–59) was placed here, seven years after his death. This popular figure was appointed to quell anti-Hungarian feeling and the statue recalls his triumphant entry into Zagreb in 1848. Despite being a servant of the Austro-Hungarian empire, he became an ardent Croatian nationalist; he abolished feudalism, waged war on Hungary and united Croatia, Slavonia and Dalmatia into a single state.

    The statue has witnessed changing fortunes over the years. In 1947, after the Communists took power, it was dismantled and replaced with a monument to socialist women, while the square was renamed Trg Republike (Republic Square). The statue was never destroyed, but kept in a cellar by a museum

Weekend café society gives a real insight into city life

The square is a popular place for both tourists and locals

curator, ready for its eventual restoration. Finally, in 1990, as Croatia prepared for independence, this symbol of Croatian nationalism was returned to its original setting, only this time the governor's sword pointed not to the old enemy in Budapest but to the new one in Belgrade. Later, the sword was moved again, pointing directly southwards to the Serbian-held capital at Knin during the war against the Republic of the Serbian Krajina in the 1990s.

These days, tourists pose for photos beside the statue and locals arrange to meet beneath the nearby clock. This is a good place to start the *korzo*, the nightly promenade that is as much a part of Zagreb ritual as the *volta* in Athens or the *passeggiata* in Rome. Fashionably dressed teenagers, students and office workers appear magically at the same time each evening to walk, talk and flirt, and above all to see and be seen. Most of the action takes place in the pedestrianized streets to the south of Trg Bana Jelačića, especially Bogovićeva and Gajeva, with their many bars and ice-cream parlours.

The imposing statue of Governor Josip Jelačić

The Market

All around Trg Bana Jelačića are elegant examples of Vienna Secession architecture, a late 19th-century Austro-Hungarian

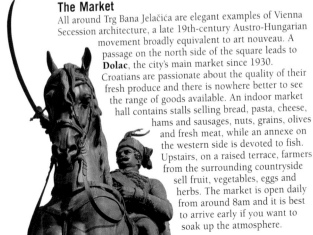

movement broadly equivalent to art nouveau. A passage on the north side of the square leads to **Dolac**, the city's main market since 1930. Croatians are passionate about the quality of their fresh produce and there is nowhere better to see the range of goods available. An indoor market hall contains stalls selling bread, pasta, cheese, hams and sausages, nuts, grains, olives and fresh meat, while an annexe on the western side is devoted to fish. Upstairs, on a raised terrace, farmers from the surrounding countryside sell fruit, vegetables, eggs and herbs. The market is open daily from around 8am and it is best to arrive early if you want to soak up the atmosphere.

TAKING A BREAK

Take your pick from the various cafés on the edge of the square. **Mala Kavana**, on the north side close to the equestrian statue, is a popular choice in a prime people-watching spot. Other good options are **Ban Café**, on the same side; **Gradska Kavana**, on the northeast corner closest to the cathedral; and **Dubrovnik Kavana**, on the south side of the square. For something more substantial, there are several inexpensive grill restaurants on the lower terrace of Dolac market.

Dolac market has the finest quality fresh produce

➕ 201 D3
🚋 Tram 1, 6, 11, 12, 13, 14, 17

Tourist Information Office
✉ Trg Bana Jelačića 11 ☎ 01 481 4051 🕐 Mon–Fri 8:30–8, Sat 9–5, Sun 10–2

TRG BANA JELAČIĆA: INSIDE INFO

Top tips The tourist information office, in the southeast corner of the square, sells the **Zagreb Card**, which is well worth buying if you plan to spend a few days in the city. Valid for 72 hours, it gives unlimited use of all public transport in Zagreb (including the funicular to Gradec and the Medvednica cable-car) and half-price entry to museums, as well as discounts at restaurants, shops, theatres and car rental agencies.

• Ilica, which runs west from Trg Bana Jelačića, is Zagreb's **principal shopping street**. Just off the square, the Vincek *slastičarnica* (pastry shop) at Ilica 18 sells some of the most delicious ice-cream sundaes in town.

2 Gornji Grad

The medieval district of Gornji Grad (Upper Town), with its cobbled streets, churches and red-tiled roofs, is the most atmospheric part of the city. It was built on a hill at the end of the 11th century and is the original nucleus of Zagreb, though little remains from that period; most of what you see today was built after 1880, when an earthquake destroyed much of the old town.

A cannon is fired from the Kula Lotrščak daily at midday

Gornji Grad consists of two separate settlements, divided by the dried-up riverbed of what is now Tkalčićeva. To the west is Gradec, the focus of government since the 17th century; to the east is Kaptol, the ecclesiastical capital, with its cathedral, archbishop's palace and religious institutions.

The most enjoyable way of reaching the upper town is on the funicular tramway (*uspinjača*), which takes less than a minute to make the ascent from Tomiceva. Take a seat at the lower end of the carriage to enjoy the views over Donji Grad as you climb. The funicular has been operating since 1893 and has become a much-loved feature of Zagreb. It departs every 10 minutes between 6:30am and 9pm, so you should not have long to wait.

Gradec

Kula Lotrščak (Burglars' Tower), opposite the upper funicular terminus, is the only surviving part of Gradec's 13th-century fortifications. It is named after the bell called campana latrunculorum, the 'bell of thieves', which once chimed each night before the closing of the city gates. The tower was rebuilt in the mid-19th century, with a spiral staircase leading to an observation gallery; since that time it has been used as a warehouse, wine cellar, café and billiards club. Those of a nervous disposition should keep away at midday, when a cannon is fired from the tower. It was first used on New Year's Day 1877 as a signal for the city's bellringers, and the citizens of Zagreb soon learned to set their watches by the sound of the Grič cannon. One man, Marijan Fröbe, acted as cannoneer for 45 years from 1928 to 1973; since 1975 the cannoneer has been Stjepan Možar.

A short distance from here, **Trg Svetog Marka** (St Mark's Square) is the focal point of Gradec. At its heart is **St Mark's Church**, the oldest parish church in Zagreb. The church is notable for its mosaic roof tiles, which date from 1882 and feature the historic coats of arms of Croatia (the red and white chequerboard, still used in the national flag), Dalmatia (three lions), Slavonia (a pine marten running between the rivers Sava and Drava) and Zagreb (a castle). Inside the church you will find a number of sculptures by Ivan Meštrović, including a Crucifixion and a Madonna with Child. On either side of the square stand the most powerful political institutions in Croatia – the Sabor (Croatian parliament), where independence from Yugoslavia was declared in 1991, and the Banski Dvori (Governor's Palace), which now houses the offices of the presidency.

From the east side of St Mark's Square, Ulica Kamenita leads to the **Kamenita Vrata** (Stone Gate), which dates from the 13th century and is the only survivor of the four original entrances to Gradec. When a fire in 1731 destroyed most of the nearby houses, an image of the Virgin Mary was found in the ashes and a chapel was built to house it inside the restored gate. In recent years, this has become an important place of pilgrimage. Nuns sell votive candles from a small shop alongside the shrine and the air is thick with incense and dripping wax.

Kaptol

From here it is a short walk to Kaptol, dominated by the neo-Gothic twin spires of its cathedral. The first church dates from around 1102, but was later destroyed and rebuilt in Gothic style. Following the earthquake of 1880, the cathedral had to be rebuilt yet again, by the German architect Hermann Bollé.

St Mark's is the oldest parish church in Gradec

Kamenita Vrata is the only remaining 13th-century gateway

The biggest draw seems to be the sarcophagus of Cardinal Alojzije Stepinac (1898–1960), a former archbishop of Zagreb who was accused of collaborating with the fascist Ustaše régime and was subsequently jailed and placed under house arrest by Tito. Since independence in 1991, he has become a Croatian nationalist hero and was beatified by the Pope on a visit to Croatia in 1998. His tomb is usually surrounded by visitors paying their respects; note also the relief by Ivan Meštrović in the north wall, showing Stepinac kneeling before Christ. Behind here, in the sacristy, are some 13th-century frescoes.

The column outside the cathedral is topped by a gilded statue of the Virgin surrounded by angels, the work of the Viennese sculptor Anton Fernkorn (1813–78), who also designed the statue of Governor Jelačić in Trg Bana Jelačića.

TAKING A BREAK

The cafés on Katarinin Trg, near the Lotrščak Tower, make good places for a relaxing open-air drink. For lunch, dine alfresco in the garden of **Pod Gričkim Topom** (➤ 62), or grab a pizza at **Kamenita Vrata** (Ulica Kamenita 5; tel: 01 481 4100) beside the Stone Gate.

Kula Lotrščak
🚩 200 C3 ⊠ Strossmayerovo Šetalište 9 ☎ 01 485 1768 🕐 Tue–Sun 11–8, May–Oct 💰 Inexpensive

Katedrala (Cathedral)
🚩 201 D3 ⊠ Kaptol 31 ☎ 01 481 4727 🕐 Daily 8–8 💰 Free

GORNJI GRAD: INSIDE INFO

Top tip Take a stroll along **Strossmayerovo Šetalište**, a promenade that follows the line of the old city walls, with benches, shady walkways and views across the rooftops of Donji Grad to the tower blocks of Novi Zagreb, beyond the River Sava in the distance.

Hidden gem Children will enjoy the **Prirodoslovni Muzej**, a natural history museum housed in an old theatre at Ulica Demetrova 1 (Tue–Fri 10–5, Sat–Sun 10–1;), with an impressive collection of stuffed animals displayed in old-fashioned cabinets.

3 Fondacija Ivan Meštrović

This engaging and intimate museum provides an excellent introduction to the work of Ivan Meštrović (1883–1962), one of the best-known sculptors of the 20th century and one of the few Croatians to have become famous beyond his country's borders. Spend any time in Croatia and you will soon become familiar with his work, which can be seen in churches, parks and plazas from Zagreb to Split.

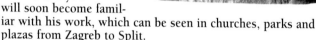

Meštrović was born in Slavonia to a family of itinerant agricultural workers. Despite a lack of formal education – he had to teach himself to read and write – his artistic ability was soon spotted and at the age of 15 he was apprenticed to a stonemason in Split. Later he studied in Vienna and worked in Paris and Rome, where he made contact with the French sculptor Auguste Rodin (1840–1917). By 1905 he had produced *Well of Life*, a group of bronze figures around a fountain, now on display outside the Croatian National Theatre.

After two decades abroad, Meštrović returned to Croatia and settled in this 17th-century house in Zagreb, where he lived and worked from 1924 to 1942. An active campaigner for Croat-Serb unity, he was imprisoned by the fascist Ustaše government and spent his later life in exile in the United States.

With much of the artist's furniture on display, the house retains the atmosphere of a family home. The main attraction, however, is the collection of over 100 of his sculptures in wood, bronze and stone, representing some 40 years of his work and providing a good overview of his style, which combined elements of classical sculpture and folk art. The most common themes are religious imagery and female nudes, though there are also some touching portraits of his family.

Highlights

- *Woman in Agony* (1928): this contorted nude figure, sculpted in bronze, stands in the middle of the atrium, a small courtyard entered from the street before going into the museum.
- *History of the Croats* (1932): this bronze sculpture in the garden is full of political symbolism, featuring a mother as the emblem of the nation holding a stone tablet inscribed in Glagolitic script (▶ 173) in her lap.
- *Mother and Child* (1942): on display in the artist's studio, this beautiful, unfinished walnut carving shows the tender features of a mother embracing her child.
- *Olga Meštrović feeding Tvrtko* (1925): this intimate portrait of Meštrović's second wife breastfeeding their young son has a Madonna-like quality.

Woman in Agony is displayed in front of the museum entrance

TAKING A BREAK

Lanterna (Ulica Mletačka 11; tel: 01 485 1818), across the street, serves inexpensive Croatian meals.

➕ 200 C4 ⊠ Ulica Mletačka 8 ☎ 01 485 1123 🕐 Tue–Fri 10–6, Sat and Sun 10–2 💶 Moderate

FONDACIJA IVAN MEŠTROVIĆ: INSIDE INFO

In more depth Although the major works are exhibited in the ground-floor studio and garden, make time to explore the **second-floor galleries**. Among the items on display are some plaster reliefs of the artist's parents, children and first wife, designed for the family mausoleum in Otavice, near Split. The original bronze doors of the mausoleum were looted by Serbian troops during their occupation of Croatia in the 1990s, making these surviving copies all the more significant.

At Your Leisure

❹ Muzej Grada Zagreba

You could easily spend a couple of hours in the absorbing Museum of the City of Zagreb, which uses maps, photographs, scale models and artefacts to explain the history of Zagreb from its foundation in 1094 to the present day. It is housed in the 17th-century Convent of the Poor Clares, along with the medieval Popov Turen (Priests' Tower) and an adjacent granary and school.

From the street with its *trompe-l'oeil* painted windows, which only serve to emphasize the seclusion of the enclosed order of nuns that once lived here, you enter through the courtyard, most notable for the fine sundial on its façade.

A recent renovation has uncovered various archaeological remains in the basement, and a tour of the museum begins with a walk through a reconstructed metal-working factory from the 1st century BC. From here, you

This early map of Zagreb can be seen in the City Museum

leap forward 1,000 years for an enjoyable tour of Zagreb's history, arranged chronologically, but with certain galleries devoted to themes such as shopping, theatres and parks.

Among the objects to look out for are the oldest known coat of arms of Zagreb, carved in stone in 1499; the original 17th-century stone figures of Jesus, Mary, the apostles and the archangel Gabriel from the cathedral portal; a set of brightly painted 'targets' awarded as prizes in competitions organized by the Zagreb shooting club, the city's first civic society established in 1796; and some charming reconstructed shopfronts from 19th-century Ilica.

There is a large collection of political and tourist posters from the 20th century, and the final exhibit features video footage of the Serbian attack on the presidential palace in 1991, together with broken crockery and furniture. If you are feeling hungry, the Stara Vura (Old Clock), a barrel-vaulted stone cellar set into the medieval defensive wall in the basement, serves good Croatian food

🚹 200 C4　✉ Ulica Opatička 20
☎ 01 485 1364　🕐 Tue–Fri 10–6,
Sat–Sun 10–1　🎫 Moderate

❺ Hrvatski Muzej Naivne Umjetnosti

This small museum gives a good introduction to the Croatian naïve art movement. Originating in the 1930s when a group of villagers in Hlebine (► 83) began painting vivid scenes of rural life on glass, the two key figures in the movement were Ivan Generalić (1914–92) and Franjo Mraz (1910–81). Before long there was a whole group of artists known as the Hlebine School. These were self-taught, peasant painters who drew what they saw, and their early work reflected scenes of everyday rural life. In time, the movement developed and became known internationally; the later generation of naïve artists, while similar in style, used greater technical complexity and their work became influenced by surrealism and magical realism.

The museum features an overview of naïve art from the 1930s onwards, with an emphasis on the Hlebine School, but also including artists from Dalmatia and abroad. The first room is devoted to Generalić; it is interesting to compare his *Self-Portrait* (1975) with the contemporary portrait of *Father Fishing* (1974) by his son Josip (1936–2004). Also here are the first works of Croatian naïve sculpture, including wooden figures of Adam and Eve and *Mother and Child* by Petar Smajić (1910–85).

🚇 200 C3 ⊠ Ulica Svetog Ćirila i Metoda 3 ☎ 01 485 1911 🕐 Tue–Fri 10–6, Sat–Sun 10–1 💲 Inexpensive

❻ Muzej Za Umjetnost i Obrt

The wide-ranging Arts and Crafts Museum is housed in a late 19th-

century building designed by Hermann Bollé (1845–1916), the architect of the cathedral and Mirogoj cemetery. It was founded immediately following the earthquake of 1880 to preserve traditional works of art and craft in the face of the new threat of mass production.

The museum's collections of painting, sculpture, clocks, musical instruments, furniture, silverware and graphic design offers a broad sweep through the arts and it is easy to get overwhelmed, but it is manageable if you concentrate on a few key themes.

The highlight of the first floor is the sacred art collection, with altarpieces from northern Croatian churches (note the 17th-century Madonna from the village of Remetinec) and statues from Zagreb cathedral.

The second-floor galleries feature art nouveau, art deco and 20th-century art and design, showing how Croatian art has developed alongside the mainstream European trends.

🚇 200 B2 ⊠ Trg Maršala Tita 10 ☎ 01 488 2111 🕐 Tue–Sat 10–7, Sun 10–2 💲 Moderate

Statue of *George and the Dragon* in front of the Arts and Crafts Museum

The Bather by Renoir, part of the collection found in Muzej Mimara

7 Muzej Mimara

Zagreb's biggest museum is based entirely on the personal collection of the Croatian businessman Ante Topić Mimara (1898–1987), who made his fortune abroad and spent it amassing art works which he donated to the nation shortly before his death. Although there is nothing remotely Croatian about any of the objects on display, it is still a fascinating collection; Mimara's eclectic tastes encompassed everything from Egyptian glassware and Persian carpets to Russian icons, Chinese jade, Old Masters and the French Impressionists. You need to allow at least two hours to do it justice. Room 1 contains some of the oldest objects, including a Christian chalice from Alexandria dating from the 3rd century BC, acquired by Mimara at the age of 19 and said to have been the catalyst for his lifelong love affair with collecting. Among other highlights are a 14th-century carved ivory English hunting horn (Room 17); an ivory sceptre used by Polish kings (Room 26); *Virgin with the Innocents* by Rubens and *Portrait of a Lady* by Rembrandt (Room 35); and a sensual portrait of *The Bather* by Renoir (Room 40). If you need a break to recharge your batteries, there is a café on the ground floor.

✚ 200 B2 ✉ Rooseveltov Trg 4
☎ 01 482 8100 🕓 Tue–Wed and Fri–Sat 10–5, Thu 10–7, Sun 10–2
💲 Moderate

8 Etnografski Muzej

The last in the trio of museums on the western side of the 'Green

Right: the Botanical Gardens in Zagreb

The Green Horseshoe

Glance at a map of Donji Grad (Lower Town) and you will easily make out the Green Horseshoe, a U-shaped promenade of interconnected parks and squares designed by Milan Lenuci (1849–1924). The aim was to provide a green lung for the expanding city, with parks for relaxation, along with handsome buildings housing the museums, art galleries and theatres where citizens could spend their leisure time. Although the horseshoe was never completed, two major sections are still in place today. The first begins on Trg Nikole Šubića Zrinskog and continues south to the equestrian statue of King Tomislav on Trg Kralja Tomislava, passing through Strossmayerova Trg, where you can find the Strossmayerova Galerija Starih Majstora (Strossmayer Gallery of Old Masters). A parallel section begins by the Hrvatsko Narodno Kazalište (Croatian National Theatre) on Trg Maršala Tita and leads south past the Ethnographic Museum towards the Botanički Vrt (Botanical Garden), an English-style landscape garden laid out in 1889.

Horseshoe' (► 56, panel) is devoted to folk culture, both in Croatia and elsewhere. The ground-floor gallery of the Ethnographic Museum features objects brought back from abroad by Croatian explorers, notably the brothers Mirko and Stjepan Seljan. Of greater interest are the first-floor displays of folk costume and jewellery from the various regions of Croatia, along with a number of traditional musical instruments. The museum is housed in a magnificent congress hall, dating from 1904, with stained glass, sculptures on the façade and frescoes inside the central dome.

➕ 200 B2 ✉ Trg Mažuranića 14
☎ 01 482 6220 🕐 Tue–Thu 10–6, Fri–Sun 10–1 💰 Moderate

9 Arheološki Muzej

Spread out over three floors of a 19th-century Habsburg palace, this archaeological museum has a comprehensive collection of finds from prehistoric to Roman times, but the biggest attraction is the Vučedol Dove, a three-legged pouring vessel in the shape of a bird dating from the third millennium BC. The vessel probably served some religious or ceremonial function, such as anointing with oil. It is the finest surviving example of the grooved pottery, decorated with geometric patterns, that was a hallmark of the Vučedol culture around Vukovar in eastern Croatia more than 4,000 years ago. Since the siege of Vukovar in 1991, the Vučedol Dove has become a powerful symbol of peace, reproduced on the 20-kuna banknote. Also on display is the Zagreb Mummy, brought back from Egypt in 1848. It was wrapped in a 4th-century BC linen shroud containing the world's longest example of the Etruscan language – an ancient text still to be deciphered. Don't miss the Lapidarium in the museum courtyard, with Roman stone monuments and a café.

➕ 201 D3 ✉ Trg Nikole Šubića Zrinskog 19 ☎ 01 487 3101
🕐 Tue–Fri 10–5, Sat–Sun 10–1
💰 Moderate

10 Maksimirski Perivoj

The residents of Zagreb flock to Maksimir Park, one of the oldest public parks in Europe, on weekend afternoons to stroll, ride bicycles, feed the swans, take the kids to play on the swings or relax on the grass. Footpaths, lakes, bridges, follies and a belvedere café all help to create an enjoyable retreat, a short tram ride from the city. A zoo houses native species such as brown bears and wolves, as well as elephants, lions, tigers, chimpanzees, crocodiles, an aquarium and a reptile house.

➕ 201 F3 🚋 Tram 11, 12
Zoo
☎ 01 230 2199 🕐 Daily 9–8, in summer; 9–5, in winter 💰 Moderate

11 Groblje Mirogoj

Take the bus to Mirogoj from outside the cathedral and you will probably be joined by widows carrying flowers and candles to adorn their husbands' graves – a reminder that this is a real cemetery and not just a museum piece.

Designed by the ubiquitous Hermann Bollé in 1876, it lies

Arcaded walkways in Miragoj Cemetery

Bleak mid-winter on Bear Mountain

behind a long ivy-covered wall topped by green domes. Most impressive are the neo-Renaissance arcades to either side of the main entrance, with mosaic-tiled floors and elaborate funereal monuments marking the tombs of Croatia's noble families.

Halfway along the arcade to the right, look out for the tomb of Stjepan Radić (1871–1928), the leader of the Croatian Peasants Party and advocate of independence who was shot dead in the Belgrade parliament in 1928. The first president of Croatia, Franjo Tuđman (1922–99), occupies a grandiose black granite tomb behind the main chapel. It's just as interesting to wander among the rows of ordinary graves, where Catholic, Orthodox, Jewish, Muslim and Communist citizens lie buried side by side, the symbols on their tombstones illustrating clearly that this is a cemetery for all the people of Zagreb.

201 D5 Daily 8–6

12 Medvednica

The wooded slopes of Medvednica (Bear Mountain) offer the nearest thing to a wilderness experience and make an excellent day-trip from Zagreb. Take tram 8 or 14 to the Mihaljevac terminus, then tram 15 to Dolje. Keep straight ahead past a couple of cafés, look for the entrance signs to the Medvednica nature park, walk through the tunnel and stay on a woodland path before climbing the steps to the *žičara* (cable-car) station for the dramatic 20-minute journey to the summit of Sljeme (1,035m/3,395 feet), with views over Zagreb to the south and the Zagorje (➤ 73–75) to the north.

There are numerous walking trails in the beech woods, and you can even ski from the summit in winter. For an easy half-day excursion, turn right at the upper cable-car station and follow signs to Puntijarka to reach a large sloping meadow. Shortly afterwards you will come to the Church of Our Lady of Sljeme, built in 1932 at an altitude of 1,000m (3,280 feet) to celebrate 1,000 years of Christianity in Croatia. Stay on this path as far as the Puntijarka mountain refuge (➤ 62), then follow trail No. 18 back down to Dolje through the woods.

201 D5 Cable-car: Mon–Fri 8am–8.30pm, Sat and Sun 8am–9pm

Where to... Stay

Prices

Expect to pay per person per night for a double room

€ under 250kn €€ 250kn–500kn €€€ over 500kn

Dubrovnik €€€

Built in 1929, the Dubrovnik is most notable for its rippling glass façade, which looks down over the pedestrianized shopping streets to the south of Trg Bana Jelačića. Some of the 260 rooms overlook the main square, and all have modern facilities such as air-conditioning and satellite TV, though the hotel lacks the character of the others in this price bracket. It's a good choice if you want to be at the heart of things, with the buzzing café life of Bogovićeva just a few steps away.

✚ 200 C3 ☒ Ulica Ljudevita Gaja 1
☎ 01 487 3555; www.hotel-dubrovnik.htnet.hr ▯ Tram 1, 6, 11, 12, 13, 14, 17

Ilica €€

This small, friendly hotel is set just back from a busy shopping street, a short walk from Trg Bana Jelačića. There are 12 cosy rooms with private bathrooms, and the corridors are decorated with impressions of Zagreb by local artists. Ilica is the best mid-range option in central Zagreb and it tends to get booked up, so reserve well in advance. No credit cards; you can pay in euros or Croatian kuna.

✚ 200 C3 ☒ Ilica 102 ☎ 01 377 7522; www.hotel-ilica.hr ▯ Tram 6, 11

Palace €€€

The grande dame of Zagreb hotels was built as the Schlessinger Palace

in 1891 and converted to a hotel in 1907, making it the first hotel in the city. Despite renovation, it retains its old-world atmosphere and oozes art nouveau charm and antique style. Many of the rooms look over Strossmayerova Trg, a leafy square at the heart of the green corridor connecting the railway station with Trg Bana Jelačića. There's a delightful Viennese-style café on the ground floor.

✚ 201 D2 ☒ Strossmayerova Trg 10 ☎ 01 481 4611; www.palace.hr ▯ Tram 6, 13

Regent Esplanade €€€

If you really want to do it in style, stay at the Esplanade. Royalty, politicians and film stars have all slept here. Following renovation, the fountain in the gardens and the art deco lobby are still there, but modern business facilities and wireless internet access have been introduced, along with a health club and casino. Fresh flowers, marble bathrooms, walk-in showers, goose-

down pillows and fluffy towels guarantee a stay here is the height of unashamed luxury. The botanical garden is a short stroll away.

✚ 201 D1 ☒ Ulica Mihanovićeva 1 ☎ 01 456 6666; www.regenthotels.com ▯ Tram 2, 4, 6, 9, 13

Sliško €€

This small, modern, family-run hotel makes a convenient choice for anyone arriving by bus as it is just 200m (220 yards) from the bus station and the airport bus terminus. There are 18 simply furnished rooms, with private bathrooms and satellite TV. It stands in a quiet street, a 15-minute tram ride or 30-minute walk from Trg Bana Jelačića. Guests have free access to a computer in the lobby if they want to check their e-mails. Credit cards are accepted, but there is a 10 per cent discount for paying in cash.

✚ 201 off F1 ☒ Ulica Buničeva 7 ☎ 01 618 4777; www.slisko.hr ▯ Tram 2, 5, 6, 7, 8

Where to...
Eat and Drink

Prices

Expect to pay for a three-course meal for one, excluding drinks and service

€ under 100kn €€ 100kn–150kn €€€ over 150kn

Baltazar €€

This long-established restaurant just north of the cathedral serves a classic menu of grilled meat dishes such as steaks, chops and burgers with a choice of chips, roasted peppers or potato balls with gorgonzola. It can get busy, so reserve ahead, especially if you want a table in the courtyard. If you have a Zagreb Card, remember to claim your 20 per cent discount. On the same site are Gašpar, a fish restaurant, and Melkior, a wine bar.

🚹 200 D4 🖂 Nova Ves 4 📞 01 466 6824 🕼 Mon–Sat noon–midnight 🚌 Bus 106

Boban €€

The footballer Zvonimir Boban, captain of Croatia's 1998 World Cup squad, opened this Italian restaurant in a brick-vaulted cellar just off the main square. Fresh pasta is the house special here, with spaghetti, tortellini, ravioli and gnocchi prepared in a variety of ways, along with carpaccio of beef or tuna and Italian-inspired salads and risottos. Both the restaurant and the bar attract a young, trendy crowd, and there are outdoor seats.

🚹 201 D3 🖂 Ulica Ljudevita Gajeva 9 📞 01 481 1549 🕼 Daily 11am– midnight 🚋 Tram 1, 6, 11, 12, 13, 14, 17

Jägerhorn €€

Steps lead to this pretty terrace restaurant beside a waterfall at the foot of the hill up to Gradec. The menu has a strong emphasis on game dishes. Starters include game pâté, game soup and a mixed plate of salami, ham and sheep's cheese, as well as slices of dark, meaty smoked bear. Main courses are goulash, grilled venison and wild boar stew, or ćevapčići and grilled chicken. The restaurant is attached to a small hotel.

🚹 200 C3 🖂 Ilica 14 📞 01 483 3877 🕼 Daily 10am–midnight 🚋 Tram 1, 6, 11, 12, 13, 14, 17

K Pivovari €€

You can come here for a full meal or just a beer – this pub is part of the Ožujsko brewery, which has been turning out Ožujsko lager and Tomislav dark beer for more than a century. Foreign beers such as Stella Artois and Hoegaarden are brewed here under licence and all are available on draught. The food is

traditional Croatian fare, as well as simpler snacks such as salads.

🚹 200 off A3 🖂 Ilica 222 📞 01 375 1808 🕼 Mon–Sat 10am–mid- night, Sun 10–5 🚋 Tram 6, 11

Kerempuh €€

This busy restaurant on the upper level of Dolac market attracts a mixed crowd of market workers, shoppers, business people and tourists, so try to arrive early for a lunchtime seat on the terrace. The menu changes daily according to what is available in the market, so the food is ultra-fresh and you have a prime view of the activity going on beneath you. The main emphasis is on meat dishes such as pašticada, a casserole of veal stewed in wine and served with mashed potatoes and pasta. Dishes are listed in Croatian only, but the waiters will translate for you.

🚹 201 D3 🖂 Kaptol 3 📞 01 481 9000 🕼 Mon–Sat 6–3, 5–midnight 🚋 Tram 1, 6, 11, 12, 13, 14, 17

Paviljon €€€

Paviljon occupies the ground floor of the Art Pavilion, an art nouveau building, originally designed for an international exhibition in Budapest in 1896, then reassembled two years later in Zagreb. With modern art on the walls and a pianist playing while you dine, this classy restaurant is definitely a place to dress up for that special occasion. The menu combines Croatian, Italian and Central European influences, from the signature dish of crispy roast duck on a bed of red cabbage with figs to offerings such as shrimps with chickpeas and rosemary or chicken stuffed with truffles and Fontina cheese.

✚ 201 D2 ✉ Trg Kralja Tomislava 22
☎ 01 481 3066 ⏰ Mon–Sat
noon–midnight ⛉ Tram 2, 4, 6, 9, 13

Pod Gričkim Topom €€

Pod Gričkim Topom, whose name means 'under the Grič cannon', makes the perfect setting for a romantic meal. The attentive staff at this flower-decked terrace overlooking Zagreb a few steps from the Lotrščak Tower, are fluent in several languages, and will bring you a small starter on the house. Afterwards, you could try the Zagorje soup, a hearty broth of ham, cheese, bacon, mushrooms and potatoes. The main menu is heavy on grilled fish and expertly cooked steaks, such as the zagrebački odrezak, a veal schnitzel stuffed with ham and cheese. If you need the toilet, remember the key symbol is for men and the keyhole for women.

✚ 200 C3 ✉ Zakmardijeve Stube 5
(near upper funicular station) ☎ 01
483 3607 ⏰ Daily 11am–midnight
⛉ Funicular to Gradec

Puntijarka €

An easy 45-minute walk from the upper cable-car station leads to this mountain refuge on the slopes of Mount Medvednica. There are no frills here, just good, hearty fare such as grah (bean stew), roast pork and purica z mlincima (turkey with pasta), served at outdoor tables in summer or in the snug alpine lodge in winter. A path beside the restaurant leads down towards the tram terminus at Dolje, so you can come up on the cable-car for lunch and walk back down in a couple of hours.

✚ 201 off D5 ✉ Sljemenska Cesta 4
☎ 01 458 0384 ⏰ Daily 9–9

Rubelj €

Rubelj is the busiest of several cheap grill restaurants on a terrace beneath Dolac market, with enticing outdoor tables and giant parasols. The simple menu features čevapčići, kebabs, hamburgers, sausages and mixed grills, served with a selection of crusty bread, raw onions and ajvar (aubergine and pepper relish). Steaks, pizzas, grilled squid, salad and chips are all available, but most people go for the čevapčići. It's a good place for a snack lunch right in the heart of town.

✚ 201 D3 ✉ Dolac 2
☎ 01 481 8777
⏰ Daily 8am–11pm
⛉ Tram 1, 6, 11, 12, 13, 14, 17

Vallis Aurea €

A little piece of Slavonia in the heart of Zagreb, Villa Aurea lies at the foot of the funicular to Gradec. Wooden tables and embroidered tablecloths give it a cosy, intimate atmosphere. The food is spicy, with starters such as ham and horse-radish, smoked ox tongue or kulen (Slavonian salami), and there are always three good-value daily specials ranging from boiled beef to fish stew. If you don't want a full meal, try a glass of chilled Slavonian wine on the summer terrace.

✚ 200 C3 ✉ Ulica Tomića 4
☎ 01 483 1305
⏰ Mon–Sat 9am–11pm
⛉ Tram 1, 6, 11, 12, 13, 14, 17

Where to... Shop

Shopping in Zagreb has come a long way since the days of Communist Yugoslavia, and the city now has a variety of department stores, fashion boutiques and shopping malls.

SHOPPING DISTRICTS

The main shopping areas are all close to Trg Bana Jelačića. Ilica, which runs west of Trg Bana Jelačića for some 7km (4 miles), has been the city's main commercial street since the 19th century and now houses shops selling antiques, clothing and shoes. Vlaška, which begins near the cathedral and continues east, offers a similar mix.

For more alternative shopping, Radićeva, running uphill from the northwest corner of Trg Bana Jelačića, has funky, offbeat designer boutiques and quirky art galleries and craft shops, such as Manifactura Miniatura (Radićeva 35), which specializes in toy soldiers and figurines.

SHOPPING CENTRES

Many of Zagreb's smarter shops are in shopping centres rather than on the main streets. Among the biggest are the historic department store Nama (Ilica 4), Centar Kaptol (Nova Ves 17), Importanne Galleria (Iblerov Trg, near Vlaška) and Rotunda Centar (Jurišićeva 19, near Trg Bana Jelačića).

The more modern centres, such as Centar Kaptol and Importanne Galleria, resemble American-style shopping malls, with eateries and multiplex cinemas, as well as shops. Most of these are open Monday to Saturday 9am to 9pm, and a few open on Sunday mornings.

FOOD AND DRINK

For fresh produce, you can't beat the farmers' market which takes place every morning at Dolac, just off Trg Bana Jelačića. Fresh fruit and vegetables are displayed on outdoor stalls, while freshly baked bread, pasta, cheese, fresh and cured meats are available inside the market hall.

Around the corner from the cathedral, Galerija Pršut has an excellent range of Dalmatian and Istrian cured ham, sausages, cheeses, olive oil, wines and spirits. Further along the same street, Franja (Vlaška 62) sells fresh coffees and teas, plus a wide selection of wines and liqueurs, while Ivić (Vlaška 64) is Zagreb's top delicatessen, with fresh salads and sandwiches to take away. If you can't make it to Istria, you can buy truffles from Zigante Tartufi (▶ 112) in various shops, including Kaufland supermarket inside the Rotunda Centar.

FASHIONS

Heruc Galerija (Ilica 26) has affordable, stylish women's clothes. For the latest female fashions, check out Image Haddad (Ilica 6), Moda Stolnik (Vlaška 58) and Charlie (Vlaška 47).

For expensive, trendy women's shoes, visit Roberto Botticelli (Ilica 14) or Karla (Vlaška 65). Men can find a good range of smart casual clothing at Camel (Ulica Ljudevita Gaja 2), or silk ties at Croata (Kaptol 13).

OTHER SHOPS

Algoritam (Ulica Ljudevita Gaja 1), beneath Hotel Dubrovnik, is the top bookshop in town, with foreign-language books and magazines, including Croatian literature translated into English.

Aromatica (Vlaška 7) is the place to go for cosmetics and soaps made naturally from lavender and other Adriatic herbs.

Where to...
Be Entertained

Zagreb has a thriving arts scene, and with numerous theatres, cinemas, concert halls and orchestras, there is something going on throughout the year.

To find out what's on, pick up a copy of the monthly *Events and Performances* leaflet from the tourist office on Trg Bana Jelačića, or check the listings on their website (www.zagreb-touristinfo.hr). Another good source of information is the magazine *Zagreb in your Pocket*, available free from tourist offices, cafés and hotels (www.inyourpocket.com). In summer look for outdoor events such as the **bandstand concerts** in Trg Nikole Šubića Zrinskog, south of Trg Bana Jelačića.

During the **International Folklore Festival** in July, folk dancers perform in Trg Bana Jelačića, while the annual **Zagreb Summer Festival**, held between mid-July and mid-August, features chamber music concerts in the cathedral and the courtyards of Gornji Grad.

THEATRE AND MUSIC

The prestige venue for drama, ballet and opera is the **Hrvatsko Narodno Kazalište** (Croatian National Theatre; tel: 01 482 8532; www.hnk.hr), an ostentatious, Habsburg-era opera house on Trg Maršala Tita opened by Emperor Franz Josef I in 1895. The theatre is home to the National Ballet and National Opera, but also plays host to visiting companies throughout the year. The box office is open Monday to Friday from 10am to 2pm, plus 90 minutes before all performances.

The other major venue is the **Vatroslav Lisinski concert hall** at Trg Stjepan Radića 4 (tel: 01 612 1166; www.lisinski.hr). Home to the Zagreb Philharmonic Orchestra, it also features jazz and other musical events.

Children might enjoy the shows performed at the **Zagrebačko Kazalište Lutaka** (Zagreb Puppet Theatre).

CINEMA

Most major international films are shown shortly after their release, usually with subtitles. Two good central cinemas are **Broadway Tkalča** in the Centar Kaptol shopping centre, and the **Zagreb on Trg Petra Preradovića**. Listings of what's on can be found in the daily newspapers.

NIGHTLIFE

For most locals, a night out, especially in summer, means finding a café and sitting out on the street. The most popular streets are Radićeva and Tkalčićeva north of Trg Bana Jelačića, and Gajeva and Bogovićeva to the south. The established place for serious clubbers is **Aquarius**, on the shores of Lake Jarun, 4km (2.5 miles) south of the city. For live music, check out **Sax** (Palmotićeva 22).

SOCCER

The city's top team, Dinamo Zagreb, plays at the **Maksimir Stadium** opposite Maksimir Park, which is also the venue for home games for the Croatian national team. Most matches take place at weekends between August and May. You can usually buy cheap tickets outside the ground, or you can check in advance (tel: 01 238 6111).

Inland Croatia

Getting Your Bearings

Although most visitors to Croatia tend to stay in Zagreb and around the coast, to do so is to ignore about half of the country. The regions to the north, south and east of Zagreb offer a beguiling mix of scenery, historic towns and authentic rural life. Travel in inland Croatia is not always easy – the roads are slow, facilities are basic and the continuing effects of the war can be emotionally wearing – but it certainly has its rewards for the adventurous visitor who is prepared to step off the beaten track.

★ Don't Miss

A tour boat on a lake in Plitvice Lakes National Park

The rivers Sava, Drava and Danube form natural borders with Bosnia, Hungary and Serbia, separating Croatia from its neighbours. This entire region has long had the feel of a frontier land, ever since Pope Leo X declared Croatia to be 'the ramparts of Christendom' in 1519. During the 16th century, the Habsburg emperors established a military frontier along the Bosnian border in order to defend Croatia from the Turks. Four centuries later, the same border became a battleground and the scars of the recent war are still evident in towns such as Osijek, Slavonski Brod and especially Vukovar.

The eastern province of Slavonia, virtually untouched by tourism, is a region of vineyards, wheat fields and villages, where people sell sacks of red peppers from outside their houses, which end up in the famously spicy salami, goulash and fish stew. The chic resorts of Istria and Dalmatia seem a very long way away.

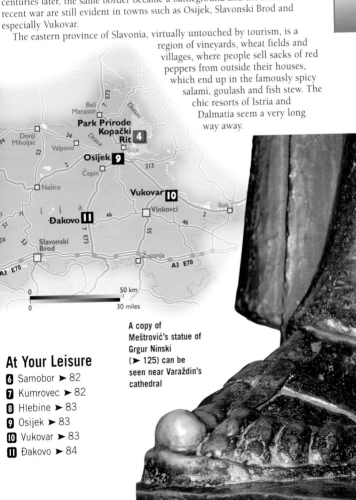

A copy of Meštrović's statue of Grgur Ninski (➤ 125) can be seen near Varaždin's cathedral

At Your Leisure

The attractions of inland Croatia are spread across a wide area and this tour involves many hours of driving on country roads, so you need to be prepared for long days.

Inland Croatia in Four Days

Day One

Morning
Make an early start to explore the **❶Plitvice Lakes** (left, ➤ 70–72). You could easily spend all day here, but in a few hours you should be able to walk to the Veliki Slap waterfall and take a boat trip across Lake Kozjak.

Afternoon and Evening
Head north along the old main road from Split to Zagreb, where several rustic roadside restaurants offer spit-roast lamb and pork. Arriving at Karlovac, take the minor road to Jastrebarsko and drive over the hills to spend the night in **❻Samobor** (➤ 82). If you still have some room, the cafés around the main square serve custard tarts.

Day Two

Morning
Take the motorway towards Zagreb, then north to Zabok to begin a circuit of the Zagorje with the museum village of **❼Kumrovec** (➤ 82).

Afternoon and Evening

After lunch at Grešna Gorica (▶ 87), you should just have time to visit the **Zagorje castles** of Veliki Tabor and Trakošćan (bottom left, ▶ 73–75) before continuing to the baroque town of **Varaždin** (right, ▶ 76–77). Take an evening walk around the old town and have a drink in the main square before a slap-up dinner at Zlatna Guška (▶ 87).

Day Three

Morning

It takes about three hours to drive across the Pannonian plain from Varaždin to Osijek, though you could break the journey with a visit to the naïve art galleries of **Hlebine** (▶ 83).

Afternoon and Evening

Arriving in Osijek (▶ 83), head straight for the **Kopački Rit Nature Park** (▶ 78–79) and book a boat trip on the Orao I to see herons and cormorants on the Danube flood plain. Spend the night in the nearby village of Bilje and treat yourself to some spicy Slavonian stew at Pod Varge (▶ 87).

Day Four

Morning

Spend an hour wandering around the Tvrđa, the 18th-century fortress on the outskirts of Osijek, then head south to **Đakovo** (▶ 84) to see the cathedral.

Afternoon and Evening

Join the main Zagreb-Belgrade motorway for the fast journey to Novska, then drive south to Jasenovac, the entry point for the **Lonjsko Polje Nature Park** (left, ▶ 80–81). Spend the rest of the day exploring the villages inside the park, then stay the night in a wooden cottage at Mužilovčica (▶ 85).

❶ Plitvička Jezera

The Plitvice Lakes are undoubtedly inland Croatia's top tourist attraction, seen by more than 600,000 visitors a year. In 1949, the entire area was declared Croatia's first national park, and in 1979 it was given UNESCO World Heritage status. In summer, it is crowded with coach parties from the coastal resorts, but come out of season, or early in the morning, and you can still have the place to yourself.

There can be no more dramatic sight in Croatia than the rushing waters of Veliki Slap, cascading 70m (230 feet) over a limestone cliff and into the River Korana. This is merely the culmination of a series of 16 emerald-green lakes, linked by waterfalls, which drop more than 150m (490 feet) over a distance of 8km (5 miles). Marked paths and wooden bridges take you through the park.

The lakes were formed from travertine, a muddy, calcareous deposit left behind by the mixture of moss and eroded limestone, with the result that they are gradually rising. This is a rare, lush landscape in a region where rugged limestone karst is the dominant feature. Brown bears and wolves inhabit the beech, fir and spruce forests, and lynx have returned.

Numerous species of butterflies, birds and wild flowers thrive here. The peaceful scenes of nature are tragically at odds with the recent history of the park – it was occupied by Serb forces from 1991 to 1995 and the first deaths in the war occurred here.

Below and right: the scenery throughout the park is outstanding

Seeing the Lakes

It is possible to spend several days exploring the national park, staying at one of the three on-site hotels, but most people come just for a day-trip. Even if you only have a few hours, the park is so well geared up for visitors that you can easily make the most of your time. The lakes are connected by a network of wooden footpaths and bridges, some of which pass right under and across the waterfalls, close enough to feel the spray.

With constantly changing colours and light, the Plitvice Lakes take on a different character in each season of the year. In summer, when most visitors come, they are refreshingly cool but crowded. The best times to visit are spring, when melting snows increase the flow of water, and autumn, when the forests take on a gorgeous hue. In winter, when the park is almost deserted, the lakes have a special atmosphere, but they are often covered in snow and ice.

Getting Around

The entrance ticket (valid for one day, but can be extended) also includes access to boat trips and shuttle bus services. The maps sold at the entry points and hotels suggest a variety of itineraries from two to six hours, using a combination of walking and free transport. In four hours, starting from Entrance 1, you could follow the blue trail to **Veliki Slap** and take a boat across the largest lake, **Jezero Kozjak**, before returning on the bus. If you have a full day, start at Entrance 2 and take a bus to the **Labudovac Falls** at the head of the highest lake, Prošćansko. From here you can follow the red trail along the shores to **Jezero Kozjak** and take the boat trip downstream, saving Veliki Slap till last. With the map and the well-signed paths, it is easy to work out your own itinerary.

TAKING A BREAK

There are cafés by the park entrances and also at the major boat and bus stops in summer. For a full meal, the rustic **Lička Kuća restaurant** at Entrance 1 (open Apr–Oct; tel: 053 751024) serves traditional local dishes. In winter, the only options are the hotels.

🔒 193 F3
✉️ 75km (47 miles) south of Karlovac
☎️ 053 751015; www.np-plitvicka-jezera.hr
🕐 Daily 8–8, in summer; 9–5, in winter
💶 Expensive (varies from 90kn in summer to 45kn in winter)

The lakes in Plitvice
are turquoise green

PLITVIČKA JEZERA: INSIDE INFO

Getting in There are **two main entrances**, Ulaz 1 and Ulaz 2, both with parking areas and information offices. Ulaz 1 is the nearest to Veliki Slap, just 50m (55 yards) from an observation terrace overlooking the falls. Ulaz 2 is closer to the three hotels and makes a good starting point if you want to explore the upper lakes and waterfalls.

Top tips If you only have a few hours to explore, **it is worth spending the previous night in one of the on-site hotels** and making an early start before the coach parties arrive.

• The **entry fee is lower in winter**, but the boats and shuttle buses stop operating in November and the paths may be closed due to snow. However, you might catch a glimpse of Veliki Slap from the observation point near Ulaz 1.

② Zagorje Castles

Vineyards, meadows and rolling green hills topped by picture-book castles and churches – the Zagorje region north of Zagreb is one of the most attractive in Croatia.

Veliki Tabor

The castle of Veliki Tabor

This 16th-century Gothic castle, built on a hill 333m (1,092 feet) high, completely dominates its surroundings, though it is more impressive from a distance than close-up, as it is undergoing long-term renovation. The basic structure is pentagonal, with four semicircular towers set around an arcaded courtyard, where occasional displays of swordmanship and falconry are held. The museum contains a fairly dull collection of maces and pikes, but it is worth the entrance fee for the views over the Zagorje in all directions.

The Story of Veronika

The first castle at Veliki Tabor was built in the 12th century for the counts of Celje. A local tale recounts the legend of Veronika of Desinić, who fell in love with the count's son and secretly eloped with him to Slovenia, where they married. When she was captured, the count had her imprisoned and later ordered her to be drowned and her body walled into the castle. A female skull was found here in 1982 and is now displayed in the chapel, though nobody knows whether it is Veronika's.

Trakošćan

The most visited sight in the Zagorje is this 13th-century castle, built to defend the Bednja valley at the border with Slovenia. Trakošćan comes straight out of a fairy tale, with gleaming white walls and crenellated towers looking down over an artificial lake. The castle you see today is the result of a 19th-century restoration by the Drašković family, descendants of a 16th-century noble who was granted the estate by the Habsburg emperor as a reward for fighting against the Turks. Cross the drawbridge and climb the path up the wooded hillside to enter the castle, a fine example of an aristocratic stately home with tapestries, paintings, armour, hunting trophies, a music salon, smoking and gaming rooms and some splendid 18th-century braziers.

Religious souvenirs in Marija Bistrica

Marija Bistrica

While you are in the Zagorje, visit Marija Bistrica, the most important pilgrimage site in Croatia. The object of veneration here is a 15th-century dark wooden statue of the Virgin, said to have been hidden by the priest in the walls of the parish church to protect it from Turkish invaders, and rediscovered in 1684 when a shining light directed the bishop to its hiding place. The current church dates from 1883 and was the work of Hermann Bollé (1845–1916), the architect of Zagreb cathedral, who incorporated an earlier stone gateway and façade into its design. You enter through Trg Pape Ivana Pavla II, named in honour of Pope John Paul II's visit in 1998, with a half-cloister featuring a pair of domed pavilions and numerous marble *ex votos* or prayers of thanks left by previous pilgrims. Climb the Via Crucis (Way of the Cross) behind the church for the best views. On religious feast days, particularly 15 August (Assumption) and 8 September (Birth of the Virgin), Marija Bistrica has a fairground atmosphere, with stalls selling popcorn, balloons and gingerbread hearts, and thousands of pilgrims attending open-air Mass in the auditorium behind the church.

ZAGORJE CASTLES: INSIDE INFO

In more depth Midway between Veliki Tabor and Trakošćan is the town of **Krapina**, best known for the discovery of *Homo Krapinensis*, a Neanderthal person who lived here some 30,000 years ago. Around 900 human bones were discovered on the Hušnjakovo hill, representing more than 10 men, women and children, the richest collection of prehistoric human remains found anywhere. The **Museum of Evolution** (daily 8–6, in summer; Tue–Fri 10–3, in winter) features reproductions of Neanderthal skulls and the full skeleton of a cave bear. You can also walk up the hill behind the museum to see where the remains were discovered. A new, interactive museum is planned for this site.

Traditional rural landscape of Zagorje

Also here is the study of Julijana Erdödy-Drašković (1847–1901), the first recognized female painter in Croatia, who lived here in the 19th century; her original piano and easel are preserved, and the room is decorated with her paintings of rural life. After exploring the castle, you can walk around the lake. In summer there is a lakeside café where you can rent a pedal-boat for a trip on the water.

TAKING A BREAK

Have lunch or a drink on the terrace of **Grešna Gorica** (► 87), looking out over the castle at Veliki Tabor.

Veliki Tabor
🕂 194 B4 ☎ 049 343053 ⏰ Daily 10–5 💷 Inexpensive

Trakošćan
🕂 194 B4 ☎ 042 796422 ⏰ Daily 9–6, in summer; 9–3, in winter
💷 Moderate

❸ Varaždin

The town of Varaždin is all pretty pastel shades and heavily restored façades in apricot, strawberry and vanilla, adorned with baroque angels and garlands of flowers. It's a gem of a place, supremely self confident and beautifully well kept, full of students on bicycles, artists, musicians, outdoor cafés and cobbled streets.

Founded in the 12th century, Varaždin briefly became the capital of Croatia from 1756 to 1776 until much of the town was destroyed by a fire. The result of rebuilding is a harmonious ensemble of baroque palaces and churches, whose onion-shaped domes and towers dominate the skyline.

This is a town for gentle strolling, especially among the traffic-free streets of the centre, looking out for hidden details, from secret courtyards to coats of arms above the doors. Sooner or later you will come to the main square, **Trg Kralja Tomislava**, with its 16th-century town hall topped by an 18th-century clock tower.

Stari Grad

The one must-see sight is Stari Grad, part castle, part manor house, reached across a drawbridge and set in its own small park, surrounded by grassy ramparts and a dried-up moat. This whitewashed, red-roofed fortress, with a beautiful three-tiered courtyard in the middle, is home to the **city museum**.

The first-floor galleries feature the town magistrate's mace and seal from 1464, as well as the original Gothic gateway to the castle. The second-floor rooms are arranged thematically to give an idea of changing aristocratic tastes in furniture from 16th-century Renaissance to early 20th-century art nouveau. Don't miss the **Kapelica Svetog Lovre** (Chapel of St Lawrence), reached along a first-floor balcony, and the adjoining sacristy, set inside a round defensive tower.

A room off the courtyard features stone sculpture from Varaždin, including a 17th-century figure of the Virgin and an 18th-century pillar with carved reliefs of saints, which once stood on the pilgrim route to Marija Bistrica.

Groblje

Arriving by car, look for signs to the **Groblje** (cemetery), 500m (550 yards) west of the castle, where there is a large, free, parking area. Take a stroll around the cemetery, one of the most attractive in Croatia, laid out by Herman Haller in 1905.

TAKING A BREAK

Kavana Korzo, on the main square, is an old-style Austrian coffee house with an opulent interior – all dark wood, chandeliers, mirrors and red velvet benches. The outdoor terrace makes a great place for people-watching during the evening *korzo*.

➕ 194 C5
Tourist Information Office
✉ Ulica Ivana Padovca 3 ☎ 042 210987

Stari Grad
☎ 042 210399 🕐 Tue–Sun 10–6 💰 Moderate

**Stari Grad castle
is now the city
museum**

VARAŽDIN: INSIDE INFO

Top tip Look out for the **Changing of the Guard** which takes place on Saturday mornings at 11am in summer. The ceremony dates back to the 18th century and features the Purgari (Civil Guard), in their distinctive blue uniforms and bearskin hats.

Ones to miss The **Galerija Starih i Novih Majstora** (Gallery of Old and New Masters), in the 17th-century Sermage Palace outside the castle gates, can be omitted if you are short of time. The **Entomološki Muzej** (Entomological Museum), a collection of insects housed in the Herzer Palace, will also be of limited interest to most people.

④ Kopački Rit

This vast, beautiful wetland reserve at the confluence of the rivers Danube and Drava is an important refuge for large numbers of nesting and migrant birds.

The Danube flood plain is one of the most significant wetland habitats in Europe, but more than 80 per cent was lost during the 20th century as a result of building and overdevelopment. The remaining area is spread over three different countries

Sunset over the wetlands nature park

(Croatia, Hungary and Serbia), with varying degrees of protection. Around 180sq km (70square miles) of the Kopački Rit wetlands were declared a nature park in 1967, but from 1991 to 1995 they were occupied by Serbian forces who laid landmines in the park. Fortunately, most of the wildlife has survived, the mines have been cleared and the area is once again safe for visitors.

Even on a short visit to Kopački Rit, you will see a wide variety of fauna and flora. Much of the park is made up of willow, poplar and oak forests, home to large populations of deer, pine marten and wild boar. The rivers teem with carp, pike and catfish, and the ponds of reed, sedge and water-lilies become great marshy swamps when the Danube floods in summer.

The best introduction to the park is to take a **boat trip** on the *Orao I*, which leaves three or four times daily between March and November from a jetty close to the visitor office. The staff issue you with binoculars, and you may see herons, cormorants and geese, or if you are lucky, even catch a glimpse of a kingfisher, white-tailed eagle or black stork.

Another option is to go walking in the oak forests around **Tikveš**, deep inside the park. The hunting lodge here was used by Prince Eugene of Savoy during the 18th century, and later by President Tito, but there are now plans to restore it as a trendy restaurant and eco-lodge.

TAKING A BREAK

The only restaurant inside the park is **Kormoran** (daily 10–10; tel: 031 753099), 4km (2.5 miles) from the park entrance at Podunavlje. There is also a café beside the visitor office.

✚ 197 E4 ☎ 031 752320 🕐 Daily 8–4 💲 Free. Boat trip: expensive

KOPAČKI RIT: INSIDE INFO

Getting in The **main entrance** to the park is near the village of Kopačevo. Head north from Osijek on the main road towards Hungary and turn right at the crossroads in Bilje, then follow signs to the park. There is a large parking area and a visitor office at the entrance.

Top tip Take binoculars, good walking shoes and insect repellent as **mosquitoes can be a problem**, especially in summer.

In more depth The nearby village of Kopačevo contains some good examples of **vernacular architecture**, with Hungarian-style houses built end-on to the road, their long galleries facing towards inner courtyards. This is part of the **Baranja**, a fertile region with close links to Hungary; to explore it in more detail, take the Vinska Cesta (Wine Route) north from Bilje through the villages of Kneževi Vinogradi, Suza and Zmajevac.

5 Lonjsko Polje

The villages of the Lonjsko Polje Nature Park, less than 100km (62 miles) from Zagreb, provide a peaceful escape from the capital, with their picturesque wooden cottages, forest walks and nesting storks in spring and summer.

The Lonjsko Polje occupies an area of around 500sq km (193sq miles) on the flood plains of the River Sava and its tributaries. Much of this area is made up of lowland oak forest, while the remainder is pasture meadows, which turn into marshy swamps whenever the rivers rise. The flood waters attract numerous frogs and fish, which in turn provide food for visiting waterfowl and white storks. Sturdy Posavina horses graze on the pasture-lands, and local farmers keep spotted Turopolje pigs, a rare breed which feeds off acorns and lives in the oak forests throughout the year.

The main route through the Lonjsko Polje follows the old road from Sisak to Jasenovac, on the east bank of the Sava. The road passes through many pretty villages, but if you only have time for two, they should be **Čigoć** and **Krapje**.

Ponies, storks – the park is home to a variety of wildlife

Čigoć

Čigoć has been designated the first **European Stork Village** because of its large numbers of white storks, which nest here in spring and can usually be seen between April and August. Virtually every house in the village has a stork's nest on the roof. The information office issues maps of waymarked walks, including a short stroll through the forest and a two-hour walk from Čigoć across the flood dike. The Sučić ethnographic museum, has a collection of domestic and farming artefacts from the late 19th and early 20th centuries (tel: 044 715184).

Krapje

Krapje, 30km (18 miles) from Čigoć, is an 'architectural heritage' village with a fine collection of traditional wooden houses, and farm buildings. Several are being restored as the new headquarters of the nature park. The typical Posavina oak cottages are built end-on to the road, with external wooden staircases up to the living quarters on the first floor. They do not have chimneys; instead, the smoke is allowed to escape through the roof timbers and the attic is used for curing meat.

Just outside Krapje is **Krapje Đol**, Croatia's first ornithological reserve when it opened in 1963 and a haven for waterfowl, including herons, egrets and spoonbill. Ask at the information office about guided walks.

The lotus flower memorial to the lives lost in Jessenovac concentration camp

TAKING A BREAK

There are no restaurants in the Lonjsko Polje, but farmhouse cooking is available at **Rastovac** (Čigoć 44; tel: 044 715321) and Ravlić, in Mužilovčica (➤ 85).

---

195 D3
Information Office
Čigoć 26 ☎ 044 715115; www.pp-lonjsko-polje.hr ◐ Daily 8–4
Park: moderate

At Your Leisure

6 Samobor

When the people of Zagreb want a weekend in the country, they go to Samobor. Just 20km (12.5 miles) west of the capital, this is the perfect provincial town, with handsome 19th-century town houses around an elongated main square, overlooked by an onion-domed church. The pretty Gradna brook runs beneath the church, criss-crossed by wooden bridges in an area known as Mala Venecija (Little Venice).

An easy climb from the middle of town leads to a ruined 13th-century castle from the days of Samobor's establishment as a 'royal free market town' with a charter from King Bela IV in 1242. More serious hikers can head for the Žumberak-Samoborsko Gorje Nature Park, a lovely region of forested hills and alpine meadows between Samobor and the Slovenian border.

If all that walking gives you an appetite, the cafés around the main square specialize in *samoborska kremšnita*, a flaky custard tart.

🚹 194 B3
Tourist Information Office
✉ Trg Kralja Tomislava 5 ☎ 01 336 0044

7 Kumrovec

This small village on the Slovenian border is best known as the birth-place of the Yugoslav leader Josip Broz Tito in 1892.

The house in which he was born was turned into a museum during his lifetime, but since his death more than 40 old buildings in the village have been reconstructed to give an idea of rural life in the Zagorje at the end of the 19th century and the conditions in which Tito grew up. The Staro Selo ethnographic museum is part of the modern village, with farmers on tractors, children on bicycles and families living in village houses alongside the exhibits. There are old farmsteads, granaries and stables, restored potters' and toymakers' studios and a reconstruction of the blacksmith's workshop once owned by Tito's parents. A statue of Tito marks the entrance to his birth-place, now housing a display of old photos and uniforms.

A short walk down the main street leads to the school he attended from 1900 to 1905. In summer, there are exhibitions of rural crafts inside the various buildings and tastings of Zagorje food in the old wine cellar Zagorska Klet.

🚹 194 B4 ☎ 049 500476 🕙 Daily 9–7, Apr–Sep; 9–4, rest of year
💰 Moderate

Tito's birthplace is now a museum displaying old photographs and uniforms

8 Hlebine

Set in the fertile Podravina region, close to the Hungarian border, the village of Hlebine is considered the birthplace of Croatian naïve art (► 54) and has been home to more than 200 painters and sculptors since the 1930s. The Galerija Hlebine, established in 1968, features changing displays by contemporary village artists, but also has a permanent room devoted to Ivan Generalić (1914–92), showing his development from early portraits and depictions of rural life to fantastic visions of the Eiffel Tower and Christ crucified among the winter snows of Hlebine.

🔢 195 D4
Galerija Hlebine
✉ Trg Ivana Generalića 15 ☎ 048 836075 🕐 Mon–Fri 10–4, Sat 10–2
👆 Inexpensive

9 Osijek

The capital of Slavonia lies on the south bank of the River Drava, roughly 30km (18 miles) from both Hungary and Serbia. The heart of the city is in Gornji Grad (Upper Town), dominated by its 19th-century red-brick cathedral, but almost everything else of interest is in the 18th-century Austrian fortress of Tvrđa, 2km (1.2 miles) to the east. You can get there by walking along the riverbank promenade or taking tram No. 1 along Europska Avenija, a grand park-lined boulevard linking Tvrđa with Gornji Grad.

Osijek suffered heavy bombardment in 1991 and the damage is still visible, but Tvrđa has recovered its easygoing atmosphere, with students spilling out of university faculties to the cafés on the main square. The square is lined with baroque palaces and military buildings, with a plague column dating from 1729 in the middle.

For the best views of Tvrđa, follow the riverside path and cross the elegant suspension bridge to the town beach of Copacabana, then return along the north bank and over the road bridge, from where the full extent of the fortress town is clear.

Part of the plague memorial in Tvrđa, erected in 1729

🔢 197 D3
Tourist Information Office
✉ Županijska 2 ☎ 031 203755

10 Vukovar

Nowhere else in Croatia symbolizes the horror of war as starkly as Vukovar. During the 1990s, the town became a byword for suffering, and its name still strikes an emotional chord with every Croat. Once a prosperous market town on the west bank of the Danube, with a mixed Serbian and Croatian population and some delightful baroque architecture, Vukovar became a battleground when it came under siege from Serbian forces for three months in 1991. At least 2,000 people died during the siege and many more were killed afterwards and buried in mass graves by the victorious Serbian troops. An eerie silence hangs over the town today, and few of the surviving Croats have returned.

The baroque Eltz Palace, with shell marks on its façade, is home to the town museum, but has been stripped of most of its treasures. A monument by the river, at the confluence of the Vuka and Danube

War-damaged buildings are a reminder that Vukovar became a battleground in 1991

history and an early advocate of the concept of Yugoslavia. With twin spires rising to 84m (275 feet), the cathedral dominates the city completely. The interior is equally impressive, with frescoes, painted ceilings and a central cupola Strossmayer's tomb lies in the crypt.

A short walk from the cathedral leads to Ulica Hrvatskih Velikana, a pleasant café-lined promenade. Another attraction in Đakovo is the Lipizzaner stud farm, where the famous pure-white horses are bred.

and within sight of Serbia on the far bank, remembers the victims of war.

Just outside town on the road to Ilok, beyond the ruined shell of the old water tower, a cemetery contains row upon row of unmarked white crosses in memory of the bodies that were never found. Some of the atrocities committed in Vukovar are only just coming to light. This is not a place to linger, but a visit here can prompt sober reflections on the tragedy of war. The town of Ilok was also occupied during the war, but has returned to producing some of Croatia's best white wines, such as Graševina and Traminac.

➕ 197 D3
Tourist Information Office
✉ Ulica Kralja Tomislava 3
☎ 031 812319

➕ 197 E3
Tourist Information Office
✉ Strossmayerova 15 ☎ 032 442889

⑪ Đakovo

This central Slavonian city is notable chiefly for its imposing red-brick cathedral, built by Bishop Josip Strossmayer between 1866 and 1882. The bishop of Đakovo was a leading figure in 19th-century Croatian

The magnificent cathedral in Đakovo is dedicated to St. Peter

For Kids
• The waterfalls at the Plitvice Lakes (► 70–72)
• The castle at Trakošćan (► 74) – especially taking a pedal-boat out on the lake
• The boat trip at Kopački Rit (► 78)
• Storks at Lonjsko Polje in summer (► 80)
• The ethno-village at Kumrovec (► 82)

Where to... Stay

Prices
Expect to pay per person per night for a double room
€ under 250kn   €€ 250kn–500kn   €€€ over 500kn

KOPAČKI RIT

Galić €

An alternative to staying in one of the big hotels in Osijek when visiting Kopački Rit is to try private accommodation offered by several families in the nearby village of Bilje.

Set just back from the main road in a quiet residential street, Galić has two rooms in the family home and four in a garden annexe, all with TV and shower. The friendly landlady will cook you dinner for a modest extra charge and also serves up huge breakfasts of home-made bread, eggs, bacon and potato cakes, included in the price.

✚ 197 D4 ✉ Ritska 1, Bilje ☎ 031 750393

Sklepić €

Local farmer Denis Sklepić has converted some of his farm buildings into comfortable bed-and-breakfast accommodation in the village of Karanac, 20km (12.5 miles) north of Bilje. With log fires, antique wooden beds, traditional cooking and the opportunity for horse and carriage rides, a stay here provides a genuine taste of rural Croatia. The village lies on a wine route in the region of Baranja, close to the Hungarian border.

✚ 197 D4 ✉ Kolodvorska 58, Karanac ☎ 031 750243

LONJSKO POLJE

Ravlić €

The Ravlić family welcomes visitors to their 200-year-old oak cottage, overlooking a lake on the old course of the River Sava in the village of Mužilovčica. Wooden steps lead up to a balcony and the guest room on the first floor, with its wooden beds, antique furniture and fading black-and-white photos. Geese, ducks and chickens run around the yard and the family keep Turopolje pigs for the table.

Busy professionals from Zagreb drive out here at weekends for a back-to-nature experience, enjoying long farmhouse lunches in the garden. The Ravlić family have won awards for their pioneering approach to rural tourism. Horse-riding, fishing and boating on the lake can be arranged, and dormitory beds are available in the old stables.

✚ 195 D3 ✉ Mužilovčica 72 ☎ 044 710151

OSIJEK

Osijek €€€

This huge glass skyscraper overlooking the River Drava was completely rebuilt and reopened in 2004 as an upmarket hotel for both business and leisure travellers. The 140 rooms are decorated in warm colours, and all have wireless internet access and interactive satellite TV. A 14th-floor spa has saunas, jacuzzis and Turkish baths with panoramic views over the city. The hotel is well situated close to the city centre, a short walk from the cathedral. From the pleasure dock outside, you can follow the riverside promenade all the way to Tvrđa, a 2km (1-mile) walk away.

✚ 197 D3 ✉ Šamačka 4 ☎ 031 230333; www.hotel-osijek.hr

PLITVIČKA JEZERA

Jezero €€

The mountain lodge of Jezero overlooks Lake Kozjak and is the largest and most comfortable of the three national park hotels. There are 229 rooms, including 5 specially adapted for visitors with disabilities. Despite its get-away-from-it-all setting, there are tennis courts, a health centre, sauna, nightclub, children's playroom and business facilities, and the rooms have internet connections and satellite TV.

🚊 194 B1 ⊠ Near Entrance 2
☎ 053 751400;
www.np-plitvicka-jezera.hr

SAMOBOR

Livadić €€

This 19th-century town house on the main square is now a delightful family-run hotel, whose spacious, comfortable rooms are filled with antique furniture, rugs and parquet floors. The breakfast room, with its luxurious drapes and high-backed chairs, offers a daily feast of scrambled eggs, cold meats, yogurt, fresh fruit and delectable pastries, while the attached café (▶87) is the best place to try the local custard tarts. The whole place oozes taste and character, transporting you back to the last days of the Austro-Hungarian empire.

🚊 194 B3 🚩 Trg Kralja Tomislava 1
☎ 01 336 5850; www.hotel-livadic.hr

VARAŽDIN

Maltar €

At present there are only three places to stay in central Varaždin, and this small, friendly hotel offers perhaps the best choice, with 15 functional, but comfortable rooms. There is a large parking area at the back, and the centre of town is just a short walk away. Breakfast is served from 6am to noon.

🚊 194 C5 ⊠ Ulica Prešernova 1
☎ 042 311100

VUKOVAR

Lav €€

It is unlikely that you will want to stay long in Vukovar, but at least there is now a comfortable hotel if you should find yourself here late in the day and need to spend the night. The Hotel Lav was originally built in 1840 and has been destroyed by war three times, most recently during the siege of 1991. In February 2005, a new privately owned hotel opened on the ruins of the old building, with 42 rooms and four luxury apartments overlooking the River Danube.

🚊 197 E3 ⊠ Strossmayerova 18
☎ 032 445100; www.hotel-lav.hr

ZAGORJE

Dvorac Bežanec €€€

One of the finest stately homes in Croatia was built by the Count of Keglevic in the 17th century. During the Tito years it was abandoned and then used as a children's home and then as a smokehouse before being restored by its current owners and opened as a hotel in 1990. This is one of a handful of five-star hotels in Croatia offering complete luxury, with antique furniture, modern art, fine food and an extensive wine cellar. Horse-riding, tennis, hunting trips and hot-air balloon flights can all be arranged.

🚊 194 B4 ⊠ Valentinovo, Pregrada
☎ 049 376800; www.bezanec.hr

Lojzekova Hiža €

This traditional alpine farmhouse near Marija Bistrica is a good example of the growing trend towards rural tourism in the Zagorje. It has nine cosy rooms in the attic, with sloping roofs and creaking wooden floors. Ducks and turkeys scrabble around in the yard (and end up on the menu) and a stream runs through the garden. The owners make their own wine and also sell home-made spirits and jams. Horse-riding and bicycle rental are available.

🚊 194 4 🚩 Gusakovec 116, Marija Bistrica (signposted from the road to Donja Stubica) ☎ 049 469325; www.lojzekovahiza.com

Where to...
Eat and Drink

Prices
Expect to pay for a three-course meal for one, excluding drinks and service
€ under 100kn   €€ 100kn–150kn   €€€ over 150kn

KOPAČKI RIT

Pod Varge €
At the rustic Pod Varge traditional Slavonian dishes focus on carp, catfish and perch from local rivers, all served with sour cream. There is also an excellent spicy *fiš paprikaš* (fish stew).
🚩 197 D4 ☒ Ulica Kralja Zvonimira 37A, Bilje ☎ 031 750120 🕔 Daily 8am–11pm

OSIJEK

Slavonska Kuća €€
On the edge of the fortified Tvrđa district, this folksy tavern has wooden benches and hunting and fishing trophies on the walls. The food is typically Slavonian, though one unusual offering is a starter of *riblja kobasica* (smoked fish sausage). Otherwise, it is best to stick to the classics, such as *čobanac* (paprika-flavoured meat stew).
🚩 197 D3 ☒ Ulica Firingera 26 ☎ 031 208277 🕔 Mon–Sat 9am–11pm

SAMOBOR

Kavana Livadić €
Samobor is known for its *samoborska kremšnita*, a delicious custard tart in layers of flaky pastry. The pastry shop attached to Hotel Livadić has the feel of a 19th-century Viennese salon.
🚩 194 B3 ☒ Trg Kralja Tomislava 1 ☎ 01 336 5850 🕔 Daily 8am–11pm

Samoborska Pivnica €€
This beer cellar is just off the main square, behind Hotel Livadić. Low, whitewashed arches give it a cavern-like appearance. Dishes include salami or beef tongue.
🚩 194 B3 ☒ Šmidhenova 3 ☎ 01 3361623 🕔 Daily 9am–11pm

VARAŽDIN

Park €€
The attraction of this restaurant is its large summer terrace overlooking the city's main park. Standard Croatian dishes and grilled meat are house specials.
🚩 194 C5 ☒ Habdelićeva 6 ☎ 042 211467 🕔 Mon–Sat 9am–11pm, Sun 10–10

Zlatna Guška €€€
Set in a cellar beneath the 17th-century Zakmardy Palace, with pikestaffs and the coats of arms on the walls, the 'Golden Goose' re-creates the atmosphere of the Austro-Hungarian empire. Dishes include the Daggers of the Count of Brandenburg (skewers of pork, chicken, beef and strawberries).
🚩 194 C5 ☒ Habdelićeva 4 ☎ 042 213393 🕔 Daily 9am–11pm

ZAGORJE

Grešna Gorica €
This farmhouse restaurant has long wooden benches, tree trunks for tables and views across the hills to Veliki Tabor. Dishes such as venison goulash or roast pork are accompanied by home-made wine and followed by *štrukli* (cottage cheese strudel). There is a small playground and some farm animals.
🚩 194 B4 ☒ Taborgradska 3, Desinić ☎ 049 343001 🕔 Daily 10–10

Where to...
Shop

SAMOBOR

The two culinary specialities of Samobor are *bermet*, a herb-flavoured vermouth, and *muštarda*, a spicy mustard, both introduced by French troops in 1808. You can buy them at the Filipec family shop, just off the main square behind Hotel Livadić. A good place to taste and buy local wine is the restaurant Ivančić, in the village of Plešivica.

VARAŽDIN

The pedestrianized town centre is great for shopping, especially Gundulićeva, with shops selling wine, leather, shoes, fashions and souvenirs. If you're after a silk tie,

there is a branch of Croata on the corner of Trg Kralja Tomislava.

VUKOVAR

A miniature ceramic reproduction of the Vučedol Dove (▶ 58) makes an unusual souvenir, and since the 1990s war has become a symbol of peace. You can also buy one at the visitor office in the Kopački Rit Nature Park. In Ilok, **Iločki Podrumi**, on the main street, produces some of Croatia's best white wines.

ZAGORJE

A speciality of the Zagorje region is the *licitarsko srce*, a gingerbread heart decorated with icing and seasoned with pepper and honey. Although edible, they are traditionally given to sweethearts as love tokens and displayed in the home. You can buy them at shops all over the Zagorje, but particularly in the main square of Marija Bistrica.

Where to...
Be Entertained

SAMOBOR

Parades of floats take place on the weekend before Lent, when people wear masks and fancy dress. The climax of the festivities is a firework display on Shrove Tuesday.

VARAŽDIN

The streets of Varaždin come alive each summer with artists, musicians and costumed entertainers. On Saturday mornings at 11am from May to October you can see the **Changing of the Guard** outside the town hall. In June, a **History Festival** takes place, with drama, music, dance and medieval jousting tournaments for children. The two-week **Špancirfest** (Street-walkers

Festival; late Aug to early Sep) features open-air concerts, acrobats and pageants. During the **Varaždin Baroque Evenings** (late Sep to early Oct), classical recitals are held in the churches and theatres.

FOLK FESTIVALS

Brodsko Kolo, held in Slavonski Brod in mid-June, features open-air music, dancing and a beauty contest for the prettiest woman in folk costume. **Đakovački Vezovi** (Đakovo Embroidery), held in Đakovo, usually during the first weekend in July, is another big event, with music on the *tamburica* (Slavonian mandolin), Lipizzaner horses and traditional wedding wagons. Details from tourist offices.

Istria and Beyond

Getting Your Bearings

Istria (Istra in Croatian) is the most cosmopolitan region of Croatia. This northern Adriatic peninsula, virtually unaffected by the wars which destroyed so much of the country during the break-up of Yugoslavia, is now a prosperous, self-confident region and a holiday playground for millions of Europeans each summer.

Cut off from the rest of Croatia by the Ćićarija mountain ridge, Istria has always been a place apart. It was previously ruled by the

Venetian and Austro-Hungarian empires, then became part of Italy between the two world wars.

Roman amphitheatre in Pula, the sixth largest in the world

Above: boats offer tours around the coast
Right: Rovinj – a maze of cobbled streets
Below: Basilica of Euphrasius

The Italian legacy lives on in bilingual street signs and alternative names for towns (Pula/Pola, Poreč/Parenzo, Rovinj/Rovigno, Motovun/Montona). Ports such as Rovinj, with its Venetian campanile, have a distinctly Italian feel, and the cuisine betrays an Italian influence, with pasta, olive oil and the region's truffles all used widely. The Italian city of Trieste is less than an hour away and Venice is a short trip by catamaran.

Not surprisingly, given its proximity to central Europe, Istria is where tourism has made the greatest impact. Coastal towns such as Poreč, Rovinj and Pula reverberate with Italian and German accents and there is a real buzz on summer evenings as people stroll along the promenades. Just inland is a different Istria, of vineyards, olive groves, oak woods and hilltop towns. To the south, Kvarner bay separates Istria from Dalmatia, with Croatia's two largest islands, Krk and Cres, sheltering beneath the Gorski Kotar and Velebit mountains.

See the best of both coastal and inland Istria on this easy three-day tour. The roads are good and distances are short, so you should have plenty of time for relaxing as well as sightseeing.

Istria in Three Days

Day One

Morning
Take a walk around the old town of Poreč and admire the mosaics and frescoes (left) in the **1** **Basilica of Euphrasius** (➤ 94–95).

Lunch
Follow the coast road south from Poreč to Vrsar and head inland along the shores of the Limski Kanal (➤ 97). The village of Flengi has several roadside restaurants specializing in spit-roast pork. Alternatively, beyond the small hamlet of Kloštar, a side road leads down to the fiord, where a couple of restaurants sell local oysters and mussels.

Afternoon and Evening
Return to the coast at **2** **Rovinj** (➤ 96–98) and explore the old town. Climb to the Church of St Euphemia to watch the sun set before enjoying a drink at one of the waterside bars. Take your pick of the restaurants (below) and finish off with an ice-cream on the promenade.

Day Two

Morning

Make an early start to drive down to Fažana, the starting point for the boat trip to the **3 Nacionalni Park Brijuni** (➤ 99–100). You can spend several hours exploring Veli Brijun on foot, by bicycle and on the miniature road train (right), which tours the safari park.

Afternoon and Evening

Returning to Fažana, make the short trip to Vodnjan and have coffee in the main square of this charming provincial town. If you have time, check out the 'mummies' in the parish church. Spend the night at **Stancija Negričani** (➤ 108), a beautifully converted farmhouse just outside Vodnjan.

Day Three

Morning

Head into **4 Pula** (➤ 101–102) to visit the Roman amphitheatre (left), then climb to the hilltop fortress for wonderful views, before relaxing with a drink on the old Roman forum.

Afternoon

Take the fast road from Pula to Pazin to begin a tour of **5 Istria's hilltop towns** (➤ 103). The restaurants around Buzet and Motovun specialize in truffle dishes, so save your appetite for a hearty late lunch.

Evening

Watch the sun set from the church terrace in the nearby hill town of **Grošnjan** (➤ 104), then have a drink beneath the arches of the Venetian loggia. Afterwards you can return to Motovun for dinner – the town is much quieter once all the day-trippers have left and is a peaceful and atmospheric place to stay the night.

Basilica of Euphrasius, Poreč

Hidden away in the back streets of Poreč, Croatia's busiest holiday resort, is this 6th-century Christian church, richly decorated with some of the finest mosaics in Europe.

The early signs of Poreč are not promising. Between the 1960s and 1980s, it led the way in Croatian tourism and the town is almost completely engulfed by the tourist complexes of Lanterna, to the north, and Plava Laguna and Zelena Laguna to the south. The Poreč Riviera has enough beds for 100,000 visitors.

Somehow, in the middle of all this, the old town survives intact, on a fortified peninsula where the Romans built their settlement of Parentium. The original Roman grid plan has been retained, right down to the names of the intersecting north–south and east–west main streets, Cardo Maximus and Decumanus. Not far from the junction of these two streets is a magnificent example of early Christian architecture, designated a World Heritage site by UNESCO in 1997.

One of the many fine mosaics in the basilica

The Basilica

You enter the basilica complex through the atrium, a delightful arcaded courtyard. On your left is the **octagonal baptistery**, with a deep font in the middle; this also serves as the entrance to the 16th-century **bell tower**, which you can climb for views over the rooftops.

On the right as you enter the courtyard is the undoubted highlight of the complex, the **basilica church** itself. It was built between AD 535 and 550 by Bishop Euphrasius, on the site of an earlier church dedicated to St Maurus, a 3rd-century martyr and the first bishop of Poreč. Some of the floor mosaics from the original church are preserved beneath the nave and can be seen through gaps in the floor.

The long central **nave**, with its Greek marble columns and arches, leads the eye towards the apse, richly adorned with Byzantine mosaics encrusted with gold leaf and mother-of-pearl. The upper panel depicts Christ, the Light of the World, with his apostles on either side. Beneath this is a triumphal arch with the Lamb of God at the centre. The shell of the apse features a Virgin and Child, surrounded by saints and angels. To her right is St Maurus, and beyond him, a portrait of Bishop Euphrasius holding a model of his church.

Top right: the nave and altar canopy

Completing the effect is the 13th-century **canopy** above the altar, supported by four marble pillars and decorated with mosaics.

TAKING A BREAK

There are numerous cafés on Decumanus and the waterside Obala Maršala Tita. A good place for lunch is **Pizzeria Nono**, near the tourist office (Zagrebačka 4; tel: 052 453088).

➕ 192 A4

Basilica
✉ Eufrazijeva 🕐 Daily 8–8 in summer; 10–7 in winter
🎫 Church: free. Museum and campanile: inexpensive

Tourist Information Office
✉ Zagrebačka 9 ☎ 052 451293

BASILICA OF EUPHRASIUS: INSIDE INFO

Top tips Look out for the **classical concerts** which take place inside the basilica – they are usually held on Fridays in summer.
• In summer, you can take a water-taxi to the wooded island of **Sveti Nikola**, a lovely retreat where the first public beach in Poreč was opened in 1895.

Hidden gem Look carefully on the right side of the apse for the **mosaic of the Visitation**, which shows a servant furtively drawing back the curtains and listening in on Mary's conversation with her cousin Elizabeth.

In more depth The **bishop's palace**, entered from the atrium, contains a museum of religious art. In the garden are the remains of a 4th-century mosaic floor from the original Church of St Maurus, which featured the sign of the fish, a popular symbol of the early underground church.

2 Rovinj

Rovinj, with its brightly coloured houses reflected in the water, huddled onto a steep-sided peninsula crowned by a Venetian-style church, is the most attractive town in Istria and one of the prettiest spots on the entire Croatian coast.

More than any other place in Istria, Rovinj manages to preserve a balance between being a historic town, a fishing port and a modern tourist resort. It is also a working town; the 19th-century cigarette factory on the quayside is the largest in Croatia and the scent of tobacco hangs in the air. This is the most Italian place in Croatia, with a sizeable Italian-speaking population.

Rovinj old town, viewed from the sea

The Old Town

The oldest part of Rovinj was built on an island, which was only joined to the mainland in 1763. The obvious approach is from **Trg Maršala Tita**, the large open square in front of the harbour. A baroque 17th-century palace on the square is home to the **Rovinj Heritage Museum**, with archaeological displays, a gallery of Old Masters and contemporary art exhibitions. Near here is the **Balbi Arch**, erected in 1680 and crowned by the winged lion of St Mark, the symbol of Venice.

Walk through the arch to enter the old town, a warren of narrow, steep, cobbled streets with hidden courtyards. In recent years, Rovinj has become something of an artists' colony and the main street, **Grisia**, is lined with art galleries and artists selling their work – particularly on the second Sunday in August, when an open-air competition is held. The streets to either side of Grisia, with washing hanging from balconies, are highly atmospheric.

The Church

Whichever route you take, you will eventually arrive at the baroque **Church of St Euphemia**, which dominates the old town. The bell tower, over 60m (195 feet) tall, was built in 1677 and modelled on the campanile of St Mark's in Venice. The rest of the church was built in the 18th century, though the façade is a 19th-century addition.

The church is dedicated to St Euphemia, a 3rd-century Christian from Asia Minor who was martyred during the reign of Diocletian and her body thrown to the lions. Five centuries after her death, the marble sarcophagus containing her body is said to have disappeared from Constantinople and washed up in Rovinj in AD 800. Since that time, the people of Rovinj have treated Euphemia as their patron saint and celebrate her feast day on 16 September .

The sarcophagus lies in an aisle to the right of the main altar, and a copper statue of St Euphemia alongside the wheel on which she was tortured acts as a weather-vane atop the bell tower. You can climb the 200 steep and rickety steps inside the tower for panoramic views.

Limski Kanal
The west coast of Istria is cut in two by the Limski Kanal, a 10km (6-mile) fiord situated dramatically between thickly wooded slopes and limestone cliffs. Boat tours of the Limski Kanal are offered on the quaysides of Poreč, Vrsar and Rovinj in summer, and usually include a visit to a cave once used by pirates and hermits.

The old town
packed with a
galleries, bar[s]
and restauran[ts]

Beaches and Islands

Locals gather in summer on the rocks beneath the church, where there are several concrete platforms for sunbathing. A better option is to follow the coastal promenade south from the marina into **Zlatni Rat forest park**, laid out by Baron Hütterodt between 1890 and 1910.

From the cape, there are good views to **Crveni Otok** (Red Island), the largest of Rovinj's islands, which is actually two islets connected by a causeway. The bigger island is home to Hotel Istra (► 109), while the smaller one is virtually undeveloped and has several naturist beaches. Boats to Crveni Otok depart regularly in summer from the main town harbour and the Delfin jetty by the marina. There are also boats to **Sveti Katarina**, an island just offshore from Rovinj.

TAKING A BREAK

Take your pick of the many cafés and restaurants around the waterfront. **Baccus**, just off the main square at Via Carrera 5, has Istrian wines by the glass and sells truffles and olive oil.

➕ 192 B4

Museum
✉ Trg Maršala Tita 11 ☎ 052 816720 ⏰ Tue–Sun 9–12.30, 6.30–10 in summer; Tue–Sat 9–12.30 in winter 💰 Moderate

Tourist Information Office
✉ Obala Pina Budicina 12 ☎ 052 811566

ROVINJ: INSIDE INFO

Top tip Watch the sunset from the church terrace or from Valentino (Ulica Svetog Križa 28), a trendy cocktail bar with cushions on the rocks, positioned so that you can almost dip your toes into the sea.

Hidden gem The Ruđer Bošković Institute's Centre for Marine Research, opposite the large parking area on the north side of town, houses **one of Europe's oldest aquariums**, founded in 1891, with puffer fish, scorpion fish and other local marine life (daily 9–9, Easter–Oct).

3 Nacionalni Park Brijuni

Roman emperors, Austrian princes and Communist heads of state have all enjoyed relaxing on these islands, which offer a superb blend of scenic beauty and historical interest, just off the Istrian coast.

Some of the islands that make up Brijuni National Park

The Brijuni National Park is an archipelago of 14 islands, 3km (2 miles) offshore from the fishing port of Fažana. Only the two largest islands, Veli Brijun and Mali Brijun, can be visited. Two thousand years ago, Veli Brijun was a summer residence for wealthy Romans; the remains of a 1st-century Roman villa can be seen in Verige Bay. Among other sights are a Byzantine fortress on the west coast and a 15th-century Venetian church containing frescoes and inscriptions in Glagolitic script (▶ 173).

The modern history of the islands began in 1893, when they were bought by Austrian industrialist Paul Kupelwieser. He employed the Nobel prize-winning bacteriologist Robert Koch to rid the islands of malaria, then he created a resort for European fashionable society. The Austrian archduke Franz Ferdinand and the author Thomas Mann were among the guests who visited Brijuni to enjoy its hotels, casino, polo club, golf course and heated sea-water pool.

In 1947, Marshall Tito chose **Brijuni** as his summer retreat and for the rest of his life he spent up to six months of the year here, entertaining world leaders from Fidel Castro of Cuba to Queen Elizabeth II of Britain. In all, some 90 heads of state visited Brijuni, including President Nehru of India and President Nasser of Egypt, who signed the founding pact of the Non-Aligned Movement here in 1956. Since Tito's death, the islands have continued to be used by Croatian leaders. It was here in 1995 that President Tuđman held a controversial meeting with his generals on the eve of Operation Storm, which liberated Croatia from Serbian forces.

You can visit **Veli Brijun** on a national park boat trip from Fažana, which run three to four times daily in summer and once or twice daily in winter; advance booking essential. In summer, there are also organized excursions from Pula and Rovinj. The cost includes a three-hour guided tour by miniature train, crossing open parkland with fallow deer on your way to the safari park, which contains descendants of animals donated by world leaders to Tito.

Feeding the animals in Veli Brijun safari park

The tour also includes a visit to the **natural history museum**. Upstairs, the Tito on Brijuni exhibition has photos of Tito with his many visitors, relaxing in his orchards and wine cellar, and hunting in his private game reserve. Tito's official residence, the Bijela Vila (White Villa), can be glimpsed behind high hedges and walls on the west coast, still protected by security guards.

TAKING A BREAK

There is a café near the harbour at **Veli Brijun**, and restaurants in various hotels.

➕ 192 B3

National park boat trips
✉ Brijunska 10, Fažana ☎ 052 521880 🎫 Expensive

4 Pula

The largest town in Istria is an appealing mix of bustling port city, sprawling holiday resort and historic Roman settlement, dominated by a magnificently preserved Roman amphitheatre.

In the 19th century, Pula was the chief naval base of the Habsburg empire and it remains a significant port today, with cranes and container ships in the harbour. Now it has become a busy tourist resort, though as most of the big hotels are to

the south of the city on the Punta Verudela peninsula, the old town has survived virtually intact.

Almost intact, the Roman amphitheatre is still in use for concerts

The Arena

Begun around 30 BC during the reign of Emperor Augustus and completed during the 1st century, this is the sixth largest Roman amphitheatre in the world. It was built of Istrian limestone and given an elliptical shape, some 130m (425 feet) across and 100m (330 feet) wide, with two rows of arches and an upper floor of rectangular windows set into the outer wall. In its time, it held 20,000 spectators for gladiatorial contests, and the arena is still used today for major concerts.

During the 16th century, there were plans to transport the arena stone by stone to Venice for reconstruction, but fortunately it has survived in situ. Most people will be content just to stand inside the arena experiencing the scale of it all, but to explore in greater depth, take the audio-tour and visit the cellars, where there is a museum of old wine and olive presses.

Other Roman Sights

A short circuit of the pedestrianized part of town will lead you to two other interesting sights.

• The **Temple of Augustus** was finished in AD 14 and dedicated to the first Roman emperor. The temple, with its tall Corinthian columns, stands on the edge of the old Roman forum or main square. During the summer, its collection of Roman sculpture is open to visitors. The forum is still the central meeting place of Pula, and the cafés around the square make excellent vantage points for the promenade concerts held here in summer.

The Roman Temple of Augustus

• The **Arch of Sergi**, also known as Zlatna Vrata (Golden Gate), is a triumphal arch erected by a wealthy family in the 1st century BC to honour three brothers who had fought in the battle of Actium.

TAKING A BREAK

Cvajner Caffe (Forum 2) occupies a prime spot on the main square. Take a table out of doors or go inside for the comfy sofas, modern art gallery and 16th-century frescoes.

✚ 192 B3

Tourist Information Office
✉ Forum 3 ☎ 052 212987

Arena
✉ Ulica Flavijevska ☎ 052 219028 🕐 Daily 9–9, May–Sep; 9–3, rest of year 💶 Moderate

PULA: INSIDE INFO

Top tips The big showpiece events take place in the Roman arena, but look out for **jazz and classical concerts** in summer in the courtyard of the castle or in the small Roman theatre behind the Archaeological Museum.

• Climb to the **Venetian kaštel**, a star-shaped fortress at the summit of the old town. The museum is uninspiring, but it is worth the entry for the views from the ramparts and the old watchtower.

• The **Archaeological Museum** contains Roman mosaics and sculpture, as well as coins, pottery and oil lamps (Mon–Sat 9–8, Sun 10–3 in summer, Mon–Sat 9–3 in winter).

Hidden gem Secreted behind the parking area close to the Forum is a perfectly preserved **2nd-century Roman floor mosaic** featuring the legend of the punishment of Dirce, with the children of Zeus tying their stepmother to the horns of a bull.

At Your Leisure

5 Hill Towns of Inland Istria

Inland Istria, with its olive groves, vineyards, rolling green hills and fortified hilltop towns, is often compared to the Italian region of Tuscany. Much of the Italian population left after Istria became part of Yugoslavia in 1945, and the hill

Typical narrow streets in Grošnjan

The fortified hill town of Buzet

towns were largely deserted until their reinvention as alternative cultural centres.

The most visited of all is Motovun, perched 277m (906 feet) above the Mirna valley and surrounded by oak forests and vineyards producing Malvazija and Teran wines. In summer, it is so popular that the authorities levy a toll on cars; if you don't want to pay, you can park at the foot of the hill and walk up.

You enter Motovun through the old town gate, whose walls are lined with Roman inscriptions and Venetian stone lions; turn left beside the town loggia to arrive at the elongated main square, dominated by its 13th-century campanile. Note the old well in the square, and the relief of the winged lion of St Mark, dating from 1322.

From here you can make a brief circuit of the medieval ramparts, offering superb views. In recent years, Motovun has become increasingly fashionable, especially during the annual film festival in late July.

Inscriptions on stone at Glagolitic Alley

(Mon–Fri 10–1, 5–7, Sat and Sun 10–1, in summer, reduced hours in winter), whose most interesting exhibit, a reconstruction of a coal mine, celebrates the town's mining history. Be prepared to don a hard hat and stoop through underground passages. Afterwards, you can walk around the town walls for views to Rabac, a small fishing village 4km (2.5 miles) below Labin, where pebble coves and beaches attract visitors.

🔲 192 B4
Tourist Information Office
✉ Aldo Negri 20 ☎ 052 855560

Another town which has been given a new lease of life is Grošnjan, which was virtually abandoned in the 1960s until it was declared a 'town of artists' and old stone cottages were rented out to painters and musicians. The cobbled streets and squares are great for strolling, with art galleries and an international summer school of young musicians bringing life and atmosphere to the town.

The largest of the hill towns, high above the River Mirna, is Buzet; from here it is a short trip to Glagolitic Alley (► 173) and the miniature hill town of Hum. In autumn you may see farmers with dogs searching for truffles in the oak woods around both towns.

🔲 192 B4
Tourist Information Office
✉ Trg Andrea Antico 1, Motovun
☎ 052 607480

⑥ Labin

This medieval hill town above the east Istrian coast makes a delightful place to while away a couple of hours, with a laid-back atmosphere, art galleries and studios, and Renaissance and baroque palaces lining the cobbled streets. From the main square, Titov Trg, pass through the town gate and climb the steps to reach the Church of the Virgin Mary, notable for the Venetian winged lion on the façade, grimacing and holding a sphere in its mouth.

The nearby Lazzarini Palace houses the Labin National Museum

⑦ Opatija

Opatija is the sort of place for which the words 'faded elegance' were invented. Sheltered by the peak Učka from the cold *bora* wind, its unique microclimate on the shores of

Looking across the harbour in Opatija

For Kids
- There are aquariums at Pula (inside an Austro-Hungarian fortress on Punta Verudela), Poreč (just off Decumanus in the old town) and Rovinj (► 98)
- Mini Croatia, just outside Rovinj, has miniature models of buildings from all over Croatia
- Rent bicycles to cycle into Zlatni Rat forest park in Rovinj (► 97)
- The Roman arena at Pula (► 101)
- A cruise on the Limski Kanal (► 98)

Kvarner bay made it the preferred winter resort of the Habsburg aristocracy, whose belle époque villas and hotels still stand on the seafront today, harbouring the ghosts of an earlier age. Royals, dukes and playwrights such as Anton Chekhov (1860–1904) all stayed here; the dancer Isadora Duncan (1877–1927) was inspired to create her most famous movement by the fluttering of a tree outside her window.

The finest remnant of the Habsburg era is Villa Angiolina, set in its own park alongside the Kvarner-Amalìa hotel (► 108). A 12km (7.5-mile) seafront promenade, the Lungomare (officially Šetalište Franz Josef I), connects Opatija with Volosko and Lovran and makes an equally enchanting walk by day or night, with palm and cypress trees, lush gardens, rocky coves and old-fashioned lamps.

➕ 192 C4
Tourist Information Office
✉ Šetalište Maršala Tita 101 ☎ 051 271710

8 Rijeka
Croatia's biggest port is a busy working city, whose crumbling Habsburg-era buildings on the waterfront, with their mustard and ochre façades, include the headquarters of the Jadrolinija ferry company, adorned with reliefs and sculptures on nautical themes.

Just behind the harbour, the Korzo is the main shopping street and focus of street life. An arch beneath the clock tower leads to the oldest part of town, where you will find the round Church of St Vitus, as seen on the 100-kuna note. Climb the long flight of steps from the Rječina River or take bus No. 1 to the pilgrimage church of Trsat, where angels are said to have delivered the house of the Virgin Mary in 1291. The church has enjoyed a new lease of life since being visited by Pope John Paul II in 2003, and it is usually busy with pilgrims.

➕ 192 C4
Tourist Information Office
✉ Korzo 33 ☎ 051 335882

9 Nacionalni Park Risnjak
When the heat of the coast gets too much, escape to this national park inland from Rijeka, with its cool beech and fir forests among the mountains of Gorski Kotar. Bears, wolves and lynx inhabit these forests, though you are unlikely to see any of them. The park office is in the village of Crni Lug; from here you can follow the Leska Trail, a well-marked 4km (2.5-mile) circuit which gives a gentle introduction to the landscapes of this region. A tougher hike leads to the summit of Veliki Risnjak (1,528m/5,013 feet).

➕ 193 D5 ✉ Crni Lug ☎ 051 836133 💲 Expensive

The Leska Trail in the Risnjak National Park is an enjoyable and easy walk

Further Afield

10 Islands of Kvarner bay

The wide Kvarner gulf separates
Istria to the north from the
Dalmatian coast to the south.
Although not as attractive as some of
the islands further south, those in
Kvarner bay offer Roman and
Venetian history, pretty harbourside
towns and some of Croatia's best
beaches. Each of the three main
islands can be reached by ferry or
bridge from the mainland, but they
can also be combined on an island-
hopping tour, with ferries linking
Krk to Cres and Rab in summer.

Griffon vultures in the Caput Insulae eco-centre, on Cres

The islands in Kvarner bay

Cres

This long, narrow island, 65km (40
miles) from north to south, is actually a continuation of the partially
submerged Učka mountain range. It
is reached by regular ferries from
Brestova in Istria and from Valbiska
on Krk. The northern part of the
island is forested and green, while
the south is increasingly rocky and
used mainly for sheep pastures.

On the north coast, at Beli, is the
Caput Insulae eco-centre (daily 8–7,
closed Dec and Jan; www.caput-insu-
lae.com), housed in an old school.
Among its projects is a hospital for
injured Eurasian griffon vultures,
who breed on Cres, but whose future
is threatened by the decline in
sheep-farming.

The capital of the island, Cres, sits
in a pretty bay sheltered by green
hills and makes a pleasant place to
stroll, with its Venetian loggia, clock
tower, town gates and Renaissance
palaces. Osor, on the south coast, is
the oldest settlement on the island
and today it has the character of an
open-air museum, with its stone

houses, cobbled streets and 15th-century cathedral. From Osor, a swing bridge connects Cres to the nearby island of Lošinj.

➕ 192 C3
Tourist Information Office
✉ Cons Ulica 10, Cres town
☎ 051 571535

Krk

Croatia's largest island is reached by a toll bridge at Kraljevica, on the coast road south of Rijeka. With its easy access to central Europe, and Rijeka airport located here, Krk is a popular tourist destination. The northwest coast is dominated by package-holiday resorts at Omišalj, Njivice and Malinska.

The capital, Krk, was the old Roman city of Curicum; traces of the Roman walls survive, along with a Romanesque cathedral and the 12th-century Church of St Quirinus, their shared bell tower topped by a distinctive onion dome. Baška, at the southern tip of the island, has a 2km (1.2-mile) stretch of sand and pebble beach, with views of the Velebit mountain range across the water. The beach gets crowded in summer, but you can always take a water-taxi to one of the nearby bays. Just inland from Baška, in the church at Jurandvor, is a copy of the Baška Tablet, an 11th-century stone containing the earliest known example of the Glagolitic script (➤ 173). The original is kept in Zagreb.

➕ 192 C4
Tourist Information Office
✉ Trg Sveti Kvirina 1, Krk
☎ 051 221359

Rab

In summer you can take a ferry directly from Baška to Lopar on Rab, the most attractive of the Kvarner islands. The east coast, facing the mainland, is harsh and barren, battered by the *bora* wind, but the west coast is green and dotted with sheltered bays and coves. There are sandy beaches at Lopar, San Marino and Kampor, but the real highlight of the island is Rab town, set on a peninsula beside its harbour. Open squares on the waterfront lead into the old town, a warren of narrow lanes intersected by three parallel streets – Donja Ulica (Lower Street), Srednja Ulica (Middle Street) and Gornja Ulica (Upper Street). The distinctive feature of Rab, seen from the water, is the row of bell towers silhouetted against the skyline; you can see them all from the only remaining section of the medieval walls. You can also climb the tallest of the campaniles for views over the rooftops.

There is good swimming from the seafront promenade beneath Komrčar Park, or you can take a taxi-boat to Kandarola on the Frkanj peninsula, a naturist beach popularized by the British king Edward VIII (➤ 12–13). Ferries run to Rab throughout the year from Jablanac, 100km (62 miles) south of Rijeka.

➕ 193 D3
Tourist Information Office
✉ Trg Municipium Arba, Rab
☎ 051 724064

Bell towers punctuate the rooftops of Rab town

Where to... Stay

Prices
Expect to pay per person per night for a double room
€ under 250kn **€€** 250kn–500kn **€€€** over 500kn

BRIJUNI ISLANDS

Neptun-Istra €€

Although it no longer has the cachet it enjoyed in the early 20th century, Veli Brijun still attracts the rich and famous. This smart hotel by the quayside has 88 rooms and suites, many with fabulous harbour views. The price includes secure parking at Fažana and unlimited trips to and from the mainland. On iste, you can rent bicycles, boats and horses, and discounts at the nearby golf course are available for hotel guests.

🚹 192 B3 🖂 **Veli Brijun**
☎ 052 525100; www.np-brijuni.hr

INLAND ISTRIA

Kaštel €€

Set in an 18th-century town house on the main square of Motovun, Kaštel manages to combine tradition with modern style. The 29 rooms are brightly decorated and there is an art gallery beside the bar. From the rooftop terrace views reach across the ramparts to the Mirna Valley, and there is a peaceful garden. The restaurant (➤ 110) specializes in truffle dishes and has tables on the square in summer.

🚹 192 B4 🖂 **Trg Andrea Antico 7, Motovun** ☎ 052 681607;
www.hotel-kastel-motovun.hr

Stancija Negričani €€

Mario and Mirjana Modrušan welcome visitors to their old stone farmhouse, reached off a minor road between Vodnjan and Barban. The house has ten rooms, all decorated individually with antiques. There is a swimming pool in the gardens, as well as volleyball, bowling and swings for the children. Bicycles are available and horse-riding can be arranged. Dinner is prepared with organic produce.

🚹 192 B4 🖂 **Off the road from Vodnjan to Barban** ☎ 052 391084;
www.stancijanegricani.com

OPATIJA

Kvarner-Amalia €€€

The grande dame of Opatija hotels may have lost a little of its sparkle since it opened its doors in 1884, but it is still the nice place to stay if you want to capture the faded elegance of this Habsburg-era resort. The cream-coloured classical façade adorned with trumpeting angels harks back to a bygone age, and the flower-filled gardens tumble down to the sea. In the Crystal Ballroom, tea and cakes are now served beneath elegant chandeliers. Dances are still held on the seafront terrace in summer, and facilities include heated pools.

🚹 192 C4 🖂 **Ulica Tomašića 1–4**
☎ 051 271233; www.liburnia.hr

Mozart €€€

Relive the atmosphere of belle epoque Opatija at this stylish boutique hotel, with its striking pink façade, art nouveau lobby and 26 rooms, most with balconies overlooking the sea. Despite being fitted with all modern comforts, the five-star hotel consciously imitates the Habsburg era, with staff in period costume, a Viennese-style coffee house, a pianist playing Mozart and rooms decorated in Austro-Hungarian style.

🚹 192 C4 🖂 **Šetalište Maršala Tita 138** ☎ 051 718260;
www.hotel-mozart.hr

POREČ

Fortuna €€

This large modern hotel on the wooded island of Sveti Nikola is a 5-minute boat ride from Poreč on the hotel's regular shuttle boats. It faces towards the harbour in Poreč and most rooms have balconies with sea views. Among the facilities are outdoor pools, tennis courts, watersports, rocky beach, a children's playground and nightly entertainment. The hotel also rents out apartments in Isabella Castle, a 19th-century villa on Sveti Nikola. Cars cannot be taken to the island, but there is a secure parking area near the harbour.

🏠 192 A4 ☒ Otok Sveti Nikola
☎ 052 408200; www.riviera.hr
🕐 Apr–Oct

PULA

Scaletta €€

The charming, small family-run Scaletta is much the best place to

stay in central Pula, just along the road from the Roman arena. There are only 12 rooms in this old town house, all decorated in warm pastel shades, with private bathrooms and air-conditioning; reservations are essential. The attached restaurant is one of the best in Istria.

🏠 192 B3 ☒ Ulica Flavijevska 26
☎ 052 541025

ROVINJ

Adriatic €€

The oldest hotel in Rovinj, opened in 1912, has a prime position on the waterfront in a corner of the main square. It is worth paying extra for a room with a sea view, looking out beyond the harbour to the island of Sveti Katarina. The rooms are comfortable and spacious, and the hotel has retained a fair degree of its original Austro-Hungarian charm, particularly in its Viennese-style café and terrace. It's a good place to stay if you want to be at the heart of the

action, with the restaurants and bars of the seafront promenade just a few steps away.

🏠 192 B4 ☒ Obala Pina Budicina
☎ 052 815088; www.adriaresorts.hr

Istra €€€

Although it appears something of an eyesore on the beautiful island of Crveni Otok, this large modern hotel is a good place to stay if you want a relaxing beach holiday within easy reach of Rovinj. The 352 rooms, including some family rooms, are simply furnished but comfortable. There is swimming from the rocky shore and several naturist beaches on a nearby islet, reached across a causeway. You can rent a canoe or motorboat, go windsurfing, swim in the pool, play tennis, take your kids to the playground, or eat in various restaurants and bars. And whenever you tire of the island, you can hop on the shuttle boat to Rovinj, which operates hourly throughout the summer until midnight.

🏠 192 B4 ☒ Crveni Otok
☎ 052 802500; www.adriaresorts.hr
🕐 Apr–Oct

Villa Angelo d'Oro €€€

Rovinj's first boutique hotel is set in a restored 17th-century bishop's palace in the heart of the old town. All the rooms are individually and tastefully decorated with antiques and oil paintings, making it the ideal place for a luxurious romantic break. In summer, breakfast is served in a garden to the sound of tinkling fountains; in the evening, candles are lit here for pre-dinner drinks. There is a gourmet restaurant and a wine-cellar offering tastings of Istrian wines, ham and cheese. From the rooftop loggia there are fine views out to sea. On top of all this, a shuttle boat can take you to offshore islands and beaches, and the hotel also has a private yacht for rent.

🏠 192 B4 ☒ Via Svalba 38–42
☎ 052 840502; www.rovinj.at

Where to...
Eat and Drink

Prices

Expect to pay for a three-course meal for one, excluding drinks and service

€ under 100kn   €€ 100kn–150kn   €€€ over 150kn

INLAND ISTRIA

Barbacan €€

The arty Motovun restaurant, just outside the old town gates, specializes in truffle dishes, from a simple black truffle omelette to more elaborate offerings such as polenta with truffles and sheep's cheese or fillet of beef with truffle sauce. Inside, it is cosy and romantic, with candlelit tables and exposed stone walls, and on warm days you can eat outside on the terrace.

🚹 192 B4 ⊠ Ulica Barbacan 1, Motovun ☎ 052 681791
🕐 Tue–Sun 11–11, Mar–Nov

Enoteka Zigante €€€

People come from Zagreb, Italy and Slovenia in autumn to visit this famous restaurant belonging to the Zigante Tartufi chain of truffle shops (▶112). It is in the village of Livade, near Motovun, among the oak forests of the Mirna valley, where Istria's truffles grow. Not surprisingly, truffles feature in almost every dish, with a choice of truffle-tasting menus at a range of prices. You can even have truffle ice-cream for dessert.

🚹 192 B4 ⊠ Livade 7
☎ 052 664302
🕐 Thu–Tue noon–11

Humska Konoba €€

This tiny, rustic inn is behind the town gate at the entrance to Hum, 'the world's smallest town'. It serves classic Istrian dishes such as *fuži* with goulash and roast lamb, and is a good place to try *supa*, an Istrian special of red wine warmed in a jug and served with sugar, pepper, olive oil and toast. The restaurant also makes its own *biska* (mistletoe brandy).

🚹 192 B4 ⊠ Hum 2 ☎ 052 660005
🕐 Daily 11–10, Jun–Oct; weekends only in winter

Kaštel €€

The hotel on the main square in Motovun has tables outside beneath the chestnut trees in summer and makes a delightful setting for an alfresco meal. The emphasis is on classic inland Istrian cuisine, especially truffles. Local *fuži* (pasta) is served with either goulash, jugged venison or truffles, while truffles also turn up in omelettes, risotto and steak dishes. If you want some-

thing different, try the turkey breast in plum sauce.

🚹 192 B4 ⊠ Trg Andrea Antico 7, Motovun ☎ 052 681607 🕐 Daily 8am–10pm

Toklarija €€€

From the outside, this looks like an old stone cottage, but it is in fact one of the most exclusive restaurants in Istria, set in a restored oil mill in a tiny hilltop hamlet above the Mirna valley. Don't bother coming if all you want is a quick snack – the restaurant specializes in 'slow food' and most people have five courses, consisting of soup, cured ham, pasta, main course and dessert. Reservations are essential.

🚹 192 B4 ⊠ Sovinsko Polje 11 (off the main road from Buzet to Motovun) ☎ 052 663031 🕐 Wed–Mon 1–10pm

LIMSKI KANAL

Fjord €€

This is one of two restaurants near the jetty where the boat trips from

Poreč and Rovinj stop, with a large open-air terrace overlooking the fiord. The main focus is on fresh fish and seafood, including mussels and oysters from the fiord, though you can also have an excellent and very reasonably priced *ćevapčići*, which comes with chips, raw onions, *ajvar* (aubergine and pepper relish) and mixed vegetables.

➕ 192 B4 ☒ Limski Kanal, near Kloštar ☏ 052 448222 ⦿ Daily noon–10 (11pm in summer)

PULA

Valsabbion €€€

Valsabbion has been voted the best restaurant in Istria consistently and has won best restaurant in Croatia twice. It is widely credited with introducing the concept of 'slow food' to Croatia, with fresh seasonal ingredients simply prepared to bring out their natural taste. If you are here, you may well wish to splash out on a six-course tasting menu – one focuses on meat dishes,

the other on fish, with wines to complement each course. The ultimate luxury is the 11-course gastronomic menu, full of little treats and exquisite desserts. There are rooms upstairs in the chic spa hotel, overlooking a marina and pebble beach in the seaside village of Pješčana Uvala.

➕ 192 B3 ☒ Pješčana Uvala ☏ 052 218033 ⦿ Daily noon–midnight

RAB

Astoria €€

Set in an old Venetian palace and customs house on the main waterfront square in Rab town, Astoria serves local organic produce and fresh herbs from the garden, together with a wide range of Croatian and foreign wines. Brick walls and wooden beams create a cosy atmosphere, though in summer you will probably want to eat outside on the terrace where there are wonderful harbour views.

The menu includes trendy variations on Croatian classics, such as monkfish in Malvazija wine and veal in Prošek, as well as grilled meat dishes. There are also apartments available, with roof terraces and sea views.

➕ 193 D3 ☒ Trg Municipium Arba 7, Rab ☏ 051 74844 ⦿ Daily noon–3, 6–11

ROVINJ

La Puntuleina €€€

Perched at the tip of the old town above the popular bathing rocks, La Puntuleina offers the most romantic setting in Rovinj, with a balcony overlooking the sea. By day, the terraces provide perfect platforms for sunbathing; at night, they turn into a fashionable wine bar where people gather to watch the sunset. The emphasis is on creative Istrian and Italian cuisine, such as carpaccio of sea-bass or sole with truffles. There is also a four-course tasting menu with fresh seafood and pasta.

➕ 192 B4 ☒ Ulica Svetog Križa 38 ☏ 052 813186 ⦿ Daily 7pm–1am

Veli Jože €€

This old-style *konoba* (tavern) on the waterfront is a cut above most of the tourist-orientated restaurants around the harbour. The interior is all faux rustic, with wooden benches, and walls covered in old farm tools, musical instruments and even a bicycle. In summer there are communal tables out of doors at the top of the harbour steps. The menu features authentic Istrian cuisine – cured ham, sheep's cheese, *fuži* (pasta) with goulash, roast lamb with potatoes and an excellent steak with truffles. This place is deservedly popular, so get here early or be prepared to wait to get an outdoor table.

➕ 192 B4 ☒ Ulica Svetog Križa 3 ☏ 052 816337 ⦿ Daily 11am–midnight, Apr–Dec

Where to... Shop

Local farmer Giancarlo Zigante earned himself a place in the _Guinness Book of World Records_ when he found the world's biggest white truffle, weighing 1.31kg (2.8 pounds), near Buje in 1999.

His fame spread throughout Istria and he is now the owner of a chain of shops, **Zigante Tartufi**, specializing in all things tuberiferous. In addition to fresh black and white truffles the shops sell a wide range of truffle-based products, such as minced truffles, truffle oil, truffles with olives, truffles with mushrooms, _tartufata_ (truffle paste) and sheep's cheese flavoured with truffles. The staff can offer advice and recipes, and you can make your own selection and have it gift wrapped.

Zigante Tartufi shops also sell other Istrian food and drink products such as honey, wine and biska (mistletoe brandy). The main shop is in Buzet, beneath the entrance to the old town at Trg Fontana (daily 9–7; tel: 052 663340). There are more shops at Buje, Grožnjan, Livade, Novigrad, Umag and Pula, or you can buy online at www.zigantetartufi.com.

Alongside the Grožnjan shop is a wine bar, set into an old Venetian loggia where you can sample local wines and truffle-based snacks. The Livade shop also has a restaurant attached (▶ 110).

Istrian wines, spirits and Zigante Tartufi products are also available from **Eva** (Ulica Veli Jože 2, Motovun) and **Baccus** (Via Carrera 5, Rovinj).

There are souvenir shops in the old towns of Pula, Poreč and Rovinj. Rovinj has a reputation as an artists' colony and in summer artists sell their works on the steps of Grisia, the main street.

Where to... Be Entertained

Summer evenings on the Istrian coast are so delightful that for most people the entertainment consists simply of being out of doors, joining the _korzo_ evening walk) and enjoying the atmosphere at the open-air cafés.

MUSIC

During the summer months, look out for concerts in the churches and squares of Poreč, Rovinj and Pula. In Poreč, classical concerts are held in the Basilica of Euphrasius; in Rovinj, in the Church of St Euphemia and the Franciscan monastery; and in Pula, in the magnificent setting of the Roman arena. Recitals also take place in summer in other coastal towns such as Umag, Novigrad and Vrsar, and jazz concerts are held in the courtyard of the town museum in Poreč.

In inland Istria, the hill town of Grožnjan plays host each summer to **Jeunesses Musicales Croatia**, an international summer school of young musicians. You can ask at any tourist office for details of what's on locally, or keep an eye out for posters in the street.

FILM FESTIVALS

Pula and Motovun both host international film festivals in July, with a mix of Croatian, foreign and avant-garde films. Ask at the tourist offices or check out www.pulafilmfestival.hr and www.motovunfilmfestival.com

North and Central Dalmatia

Getting Your Bearings

Dalmatia appears on the map as a long, thin coastal strip between the Adriatic and the Dinaric Alps. This is where you will find some of the most familiar images of Croatia – harbour towns dominated by Venetian-style campaniles, lavender-scented islands fringed by impossibly blue seas.

The northern islands around Zadar are some of the most unspoiled in the Adriatic, while further south, around Split, islands such as Brač and especially Hvar are growing increasingly fashionable with visitors.

★ Don't Miss

At Your Leisure

Zadar's cathedral bell tower

Historically, Dalmatia has always been separate from Croatia and the region bears the hallmarks of its conquerors. The Greeks established trading colonies at Hvar (Pharos) and Vis (Issa), introducing vineyards still in use today. The Romans built a city at Salona; the emperor Diocletian was born here and later retired to Split, where his palace forms the nucleus of the modern city. The Venetians ruled Dalmatia for almost 400 years, leaving behind beautiful churches and theatres at Šibenik, Trogir and Hvar. More recently, northern Dalmatia became a battleground during the war of 1991–5, when Serbian troops established the Republic of the Serbian Krajina at Knin, cutting off Dalmatia from the rest of Croatia. The villages inland from Zadar and Šibenik were largely abandoned during the war and still have a ghostly feel about them today.

Touring in Dalmatia is relatively easy. Most of the main sights are on the Magistrala coastal highway, while regular car and passenger ferries connect each of the islands to the mainland.

View of Skradin
in the Krka
National Park

From stunning natural scenery to laid-back island beaches, central Dalmatia has it all. The islands of Brač and Hvar are very popular in summer, so expect long waits for the ferries and arrive in plenty of time.

North and Central Dalmatia in Four Days

Day One

Morning

Make an early start to explore **1** Nationalni Park Krka (➤ 118–119), walking around the waterfalls and taking the boat trip upriver to the monastery at Visovac and lunch at Roški Slap.

Afternoon and Evening

Drive down to **10** Šibenik (➤ 134) to visit the cathedral, then take the coast road to the medieval town of **2** Trogir (➤ 120–122). Enjoy a sunset drink at one of the cafés on the Riva, then stroll around the old town before dinner.

Day Two

Morning

Don't leave Trogir without seeing the cathedral, with its magnificent carved Romanesque portal. Afterwards, you can make the short journey by car or local bus to **3** Split (left, ➤ 123–125).

Afternoon and Evening

Take your time admiring the ruins of Diocletian's Palace, then stroll around the harbour and climb to the Marjan peninsula for woodland walks and sea views. Pause on the way down at Caffe Vidilica, whose terrace offers panoramic views over the city. Later, you can observe the evening *korzo* from a waterfront bar on the Riva. After dinner at Kod Jože (► 139), it is a short walk to the bus station for the ride back to Trogir.

Day Three

Morning

Return to Split and head down to the harbour to catch the ferry to Supetar on **4** **Brač** (► 126–128). From here, you can make a scenic tour of the island on your way to the south coast. Take the road through the pine woods to the summit of Vidova Gora for views over Brač and Hvar. If you are feeling hungry, there is a restaurant at the summit.

Afternoon and Evening

Continue to Bol and walk along the promenade to Zlatni Rat (left) for a lazy afternoon on the beach. A 4km (2.5-mile) clifftop path leads to Murvica, where you will find Konoba Marija, one of Dalmatia's most spectacularly sited restaurants (► 138).

Day Four

Morning

n summer, take a taxi or excursion boat from Bol to Jelsa on **5** **Hvar** ► 129–132), where you can pick up a bus to Hvar town (below). Otherwise the best way of getting between the islands s to return to Split and ake the ferry to Hvar town or Stari Grad. If you want to drive, you must go to Stari Grad; cars are not allowed o disembark at Hvar town.

Afternoon and Evening

Spend the rest of the day soaking up the atmosphere of Hvar town, climbing to its citadel and relaxing on ts beaches. If you can, take in a performance at the Hvarsko Kazalište (Hvar Theatre, ► 140), one of the oldest in Europe.

⓪ Nacionalni Park Krka

If you make only one trip away from the Dalmatian coast, it should be to the Krka National Park. Here, you can swim beneath cascading waterfalls and take a boat trip through a limestone canyon to visit a remote island monastery.

The Krka River runs for 72km (48 miles) from its source in the foothills of the Dinaric mountains near Knin to its mouth at Šibenik. For much of its length, it flows through narrow gorges, forming waterfalls and lakes rivalling those at Plitvice (➤ 70–72) for their beauty.

You can visit the park by bus from **Šibenik**, or on an organized excursion from one of the coastal resorts. The classic approach is from the waterfront village of Skradin, where national park boats (included in the entry fee) ferry you into the park along a wooded gorge. The boats arrive near a wooden footbridge beneath the falls at **Skradinski Buk**, the most dramatic sight in the park, which drop 45m (147 feet)

Above: the monastery on Lake Visovac houses a museum

Above right: the shallows of the waterfalls at Skradinski Buk

in a series of 17 steps. In summer, you are allowed to swim in the shallow pool at the base of the falls. From here, an easy two-hour circuit leads on foot around the cascades.

The alternative entrance is via **Lozovac**, where there is a large parking area and shuttle buses ferrying visitors to the top of the falls. This is a spectacular journey, with superb views over the river. It is still possible to make the two-hour walking circuit of the falls. Between November and March, when the boats and buses do not operate, the only way in is via Lozovac; you can take your car all the way to Skradinski Buk and park near the top of the waterfalls.

Boat Trips

A kiosk near the shuttle bus terminus sells tickets in summer for additional boat trips along the **Krka canyon**. The shortest journey (2 hours return) is to Visovac, a Franciscan monastery founded on a rocky islet in the river in 1445. The museum contains an illustrated 15th-century Croatian version of *Aesop's Fables*, one of only three such books in the world (the others are in Oxford and Venice). Some of the boat trips (4 hours) continue to Roški Slap, a second set of waterfalls with a height of 25m (82 feet).

TAKING A BREAK

There are cafés at Roški Slap and Skradinski Buk, both at the top and bottom of the falls. **Kristijan**, in an old stone mill above the jetty at Roški Slap, serves excellent cured ham, cheese and olives and also sells home-made wine and brandy.

➕ 198 C4
✉ 12km (7.5 miles) north of Šibenik ☎ 022 217720; www.npkrka.hr
🕐 Daily 8–8, in summer; 9–5, in winter 💲 Expensive (varies from 20kn in winter to 60kn in summer)

NACIONALNI PARK KRKA: INSIDE INFO

In more depth You can take a second boat trip upstream from Roški Slap to the **Krka Orthodox monastery**, cruising through a dramatic canyon in the less visited northern reaches of the park. It may be possible to combine this with the excursion to Roški Slap (allow 6 hours in total), but it will probably mean spending a second day in the park and driving to Roški Slap to begin the journey.

② Trogir

Trogir is one of the gems of the Dalmatian coast. Founded by Greek settlers in the 3rd century BC on an oval-shaped island, and separated from the mainland by a narrow channel, today it is a laid-back town of cafés, yachts and car-free streets, with a beautiful cathedral at its heart.

The old town is connected to the mainland by a bridge, giving easy access to the 17th-century **Kopnena Vrata** (Land Gate), an archway topped by a statue of St John of Trogir, a 12th-century bishop by the name of Giovanni Orsini who is considered the patron saint and protector of the town.

From here you enter a maze of narrow streets and cobbled lanes, full of trendy shops, restaurants and art galleries. This is a town for strolling around, looking for architectural details as you stumble across courtyards, churches and palaces. The

On the
waterfront

one unmissable sight is the **cathedral**, begun in the 13th century and adorned with a Venetian Gothic campanile which was added in various stages up to the 16th century. The west portal, carved in 1240 by Master Radovan, is perhaps the finest piece of Romanesque art in Croatia – a riot of saints and angels mixed with scenes from everyday life and the seasons of the calendar, illustrated through rural activities such as the grape harvest and the annual pig slaughter. The upper archway depicts the Nativity, while the pillars to either side feature Adam and Eve standing on a pair of lions. There are more treasures inside the cathedral, including a 13th-century octagonal stone pulpit, carved wooden

The west portal of Trogir cathedral

choirstalls and the 15th-century chapel of St John of Trogir, with its sculpted angels and cherubs, scallop-shell niches and elaborate carved sarcophagus.

Alongside the cathedral, the town hall displays a plaque recording Trogir's designation as a UNESCO World Heritage Site in 1997. Across the square is a Venetian loggia, once used as the town court, with a 15th-century relief of Justice by Nikola Firentinac, the architect of St John's chapel.

Gradska, the main street, leads down to the **Gradska Vrata** (Town Gate) and gives access to the **Riva**, a pleasant promenade with views across the water to the island of Čiovo. From here you can make a complete circuit of the island, passing the 15th-century Kamerlengo fortress.

TAKING A BREAK

There are numerous cafés and ice-cream parlours on the **Riva** and in the streets and squares around the cathedral.

➕ 199 D3
Tourist Information Office
✉ Trg Ivana Pavla II
☎ 021 881412

The parapets of the Kamerlengo fortress, built as the residence for the Venetian governor

---

TROGIR: INSIDE INFO

Top tips Arriving by car, drive over the bridge to **Čiovo** and park on the far side, then walk back to Trogir with fine views of the old town on its island as you approach.

• Climb the tower of the **Kamerlengo fortress** (daily 9–7 in summer) for the best views over the town.

• Trogir makes a good base for visiting **Split** (► 123–125), with hourly departures on bus No. 37 from the bus station beside the bridge to the old town.

• **Ferries** leave from the Riva in summer for the peaceful islands and bays of Veli Drvenik and Mali Drvenik.

Hidden gem Look above the portal of the Dominican church on the Riva to see a **carved relief of the Madonna**, accompanied by Mary Magdalene, naked apart from her hair flowing down to her feet.

3 Split

Croatia's second city is built around
the ruins of the Roman emperor
Diocletian's palace, dating from the
3rd century. Cruise ships and
ferries come and go in the harbour,
the main point of departure for the
Dalmatian islands.

Many visitors get their first view of Split as they sail into the
harbour, with the palm trees and terrace cafés of the waterfront Riva seen against a backdrop of tower blocks in the
expanding modern city. This image perfectly captures the
appeal of Split, a lively port city with an intriguing blend of
ancient monuments and modern life. Nowhere is this more
true than in the heart of the city, inside the walls of
Diocletian's palace.

Diocletian's Palace

Diocletian (AD 245–c312) was born in Salona, the son of
slaves, but rose to become emperor of Rome at the age of 39.
He was notorious for his persecution of Christians; among
those martyred under his rule were St Maurus, bishop of
Poreč (► 94) and St Euphemia, patron saint of Rovinj

**Above: cafés in
front of
Diocletian's
Palace**

**Top: view of
the town from
across the
harbour**

Other Sights
• The western gate of the palace leads to Narodni Trg, which became the main square of the city after it expanded beyond the Roman walls in the 14th century. This paved square, with its open-air cafés, stands at the heart of a pedestrianized shopping district. The 15th-century town hall holds the Ethnographic Museum (Mon–Fri 10–3), with displays of traditional Dalmatian folk costumes.
• Climb the steps on Senjska at the west end of the Riva to reach the Marjan peninsula, a green hill with woodland walks, hermitage chapels and caves, and views out to sea to the islands of Šolta, Brač, Hvar and Vis. For a two-hour round walk, follow the clifftop path for 2km (1.2 miles) to the chapel of St Hieronymus and return via the summit at Telegrin (178m/584 feet). There is a small zoo and natural history museum near the summit. On the way down, stop at Caffe Vidilica, whose terrace has views over the city and port.

(► 97). An innovative ruler, Diocletian divided up the empire and introduced the concept of retirement, returning to his native Dalmatia in 305 and living out his later years in this garrison town, surrounded by the walls and towers of a splendid imperial palace which he had commissioned for the purpose.

Ancient stone figures in Diocletian's Palace

As early as the 7th century, people fleeing Salona took refuge in the palace, and it has provided a home for local families ever since. These days little of the original remains and a lot imagination is needed to make out the shape of the original Roman palace.

You enter from the Riva through the **Bronze Gate**, which gives access to the Podrum or underground chambers (open Mon–Sat 9–6), which were probably used to detain prisoners. This is the best surviving part of the original palace and it gives a good idea of the ground plan, as these rooms stood directly beneath the imperial quarters above.

From the gallery you can climb the steps to the **Peristyle**, the central courtyard of the palace and main square of the palace complex. The black granite sphinx, guarding the emperor's mausoleum, dates from 1500 BC and was one of 12 sphinxes from ancient Egypt that once stood here; the rest were beheaded by Christians who saw them as symbols of the pagan emperor. The octagonal mausoleum was transformed in the 7th century into a cathedral (daily 8–7, Jul–Sep; 8–12, 4–7, May and Oct; Mon–Sat 8–12, 4–7; rest of the year), now housing an extraordinary blend of Roman, Romanesque and

Gothic architecture. Reliefs of chariot races can be seen around the dome, together with portraits of Diocletian and his wife. There are altars to the saints Domnius and Anastasius, both martyred by Diocletian and now honoured in his cemetery. You can climb the adjoining bell tower for views over the port and the palace complex.

A lane opposite the cathedral leads to the Roman Temple of Jupiter, now the **Baptistery**, whose 11th-century font is adorned with a relief of King Zvonimir, said to be the first European king immortalized in stone. Follow the Cardo, the main north–south axis of the palace, and leave through the Golden Gate, beyond which you will find a huge bronze sculpture by Ivan Meštrović

The clock tower and Iron Gate, from Narodni Trg

(➤ 52–53). It depicts Grgur Ninski (Gregory of Nin), a 9th-century bishop who campaigned for the use of Croatian and Glagolitic scripts to replace Latin in churches. There are copies of the statue in Varaždin and in Nin itself, but this is the original.

TAKING A BREAK

The **waterfront cafés** on the Riva make a good place to relax at any time of day.

➕ 199 D3

Tourist Information Office
✉ Crkvica Svetog Roka, Peristil ☎ 021 345606; www.visitsplit.com

SPLIT: INSIDE INFO

Top tip The city's main **food market** stands just outside the Silver (eastern) Gate of Diocletian's palace and is a good place to buy fresh fruit, vegetables, bread and cheese.

In more depth The **Archaeological Museum** (Tue–Fri 9–2, Sat–Sun 9–1; 9–noon, 5–8, Jun–Oct), a short walk north of central Split, is the oldest museum in Croatia. It features Greek and Roman objects, including wine jars and oil lamps from Vis, and marble figures of the Roman gods Bacchus and Diana, plus jewellery, pottery and grave goods from the Roman city of Salona (➤ 135).

❹ Brač

The largest island off the Dalmatian coast, Brač is a place of superlatives – from the highest mountain in the Adriatic you look down on Croatia's most famous beach – and it is easily reached by ferry in under an hour from Split.

The most popular way of getting to Brač is on the regular car ferry from Split to Supetar. In summer, there are fast catamarans which make the journey direct from Split to Bol on the south coast. Ferries also run throughout the year from Makarska on the mainland to Sumartin on the eastern tip of

the island. In addition, Brač is the only Adriatic island with its own airport, with connecting flights to Zagreb in summer.

Its easy accessibility means that Brač attracts the crowds, but out of season it is a peaceful island of vineyards, orchards and fishing villages hiding in sheltered bays. The island is famous for its white limestone, which has been quarried here since Roman times and used in buildings as diverse as Diocletian's palace in Split and the White House in Washington DC. Even today, you will notice that many of the houses on Brač, built from the local stone, seem to have an extra sheen.

Most visitors will arrive in **Supetar**, the largest town on the island, but little more than a village with low-rise houses around the harbour. There is plenty of activity by the port when the ferries come in, but at other times this is a sleepy place, where many people from Split have their summer

Above: the triangular expanse of Zlatni Rat beach near Bol

homes. Most of the hotels are to the west of town, where several pebble beaches face across the water towards Split.

The main road crosses the island from north to south, with a side road leading up through the pine woods to the summit of **Vidova Gora** (778m/2,552 feet), the highest mountain on any of the Adriatic islands. The peak is marked by a white stone cross; from here there are fabulous views over Zlatni Rat beach to the islands of Hvar and Korčula. It is also possible to hike up here from Bol on a well-marked path.

Top: coastal views from the Bol to Murvica road

Bol

Bol nestles beneath the southern slopes of Vidova Gora and is the only town on the south coast. Throughout summer, this is where the action is, with day-trippers from Hvar flocking to its beaches and tour operators advertising boat trips, windsurfing, sailing, scuba diving and free climbing (rock climbing without ropes and equipment).

The attraction here is **Zlatni Rat** (Golden Cape or Horn), easily the most photographed beach in Croatia, on a triangular spit of fine shingle which juts 300m (985 feet) out to sea, with shady pine woods at its centre. You can get there by walking along the 2km (1.2-mile) promenade that leads to the west from the harbour at Bol. Zlatni Rat is deservedly popular and it does get extremely busy in summer; to escape the crowds, you'll have to head for the rocky coves beyond, but note that some are frequented by naturists.

Dragon's Cave

Beyond Zlatni Rat, an unmade road leads along the clifftop, arriving after 4km (2.5 miles) in the village of **Murvica**, where you will find the Konoba Marija restaurant (➤ 138). In the hills above Murvica is the extraordinary **Zmajeva Špilja** (Dragon's Cave), where dragons and mythical creatures have been carved into the rock, probably by 16th-century monks who sheltered here before founding the hermitage at Blaca. To visit the cave, call the guide on his mobile (tel: 091 514 9787) and he will arrange to meet you at the restaurant if he is free. It is possible to get there on your own, but you will have to make do with staring at the carvings from outside the gate. Climb the path to the top of the village and follow the red arrows east for about an hour. It's a gentle ascent at first, but is followed by a steep climb up the hillside to a ruined 18th-century monastery. From here, the Dragon's Cave is now about 200m (220 yards) to your left.

Enjoying the view at Zlatni Rat

TAKING A BREAK

There are plenty of cafés beside the harbour in **Bol** and on the beach at **Zlatni Rat** in summer. For lunch with a particularly good view, try **Konoba Marija** (➤ 138) or Vidova Gora (daily 10am–midnight, in summer; tel: 021 549061), on the summit of Vidova Gora.

✚ 199 E2

Tourist Information Office
✉ Porat Bolskih Pomoraca, Bol ☎ 021 635638

BRAČ: INSIDE INFO

Top tip Zlatni Rat may get all the attention, but the island's only sandy beach is at **Lovrečina**, 5km (3 miles) from the village of Postira on the north coast.

Hidden gem The 16th-century **hermitage at Blaca** can be reached on a 12km (7.5-mile) coastal path from Zlatni Rat or a rough track leading off the road to Vidova Gora. In summer, local tour operators offer boat trips to Blaca Bay, followed by a short uphill hike to the monastery.

In more depth For a **scenic tour of northwest Brač**, take the coast road from Supetar to Sutivan, then head inland to the pretty village of Ložišća, high above a gorge. The main road continues down to the sea at Milna, set in a sheltered bay where yachts are often moored in summer. To return to Supetar, turn left in Ložišća and follow the narrow ridge to Nerežišća, passing marble quarries on the way.

5 Hvar

Hvar is among the most appealing of the Adriatic islands, blessed with a mild climate and covered with vineyards and lavender fields. Its capital, Hvar town, has become the most fashionable spot on the entire Dalmatian coast.

The island of Hvar is a long, thin strip with a limestone ridge running along its centre and steep cliffs tumbling down towards isolated beaches and coves. In spring and early summer, the island is a blaze of colour and the soothing scent

Fragrant fields of lavender, commercially grown on the limestone soil, scent the air around Hvar town

of lavender hangs in the air and wafts on the sea breeze. Even by Croatian standards, Hvar has a pleasing climate; with more hours of sunshine than anywhere else in the Adriatic.

The closest access from the mainland is the car ferry from Drvenik to Sucuraj, though this is followed by a long drive across the island to reach Hvar town. Alternatively, you can take the ferry from Split to Stari Grad, the old capital. Other options for foot passengers are a ferry from Split directly to Hvar town, or a fast catamaran from Split to Jelsa in summer.

Hvar town

The best way to arrive in Hvar town is by sea, from where it appears as a jumble of brown stone houses crowded around the shores of the bay, overlooked by its old castle and medieval walls. During the summer months, the port is a hive of activity, with sleek yachts moored in the harbour, ferries disembarking passengers and taxi-boats taking sunbathers to the offshore islands. Although it has its monuments, this is really a town for relaxing more than anything else and the evening *korzo* is one of the liveliest in Croatia.

Café life focuses on **Trg Svetog Stjepana**, a Venetian-style piazza which opens out to the sea, with flagstoned paving and a 16th-century well. The west end is dominated by the cathedral and its four-floor campanile; notice how the number of arched windows increases with each floor. At the seaward end of the square, beside the inner harbour, is the **Venetian arsenal**, built to allow entire galleys to be carried inside for repairs. The top floor houses one of Europe's oldest public theatres, which opened in 1612 and is still in use today.

Across the square, beyond the Renaissance palaces of the 16th-century nobility, steps lead up to the **Citadel** (daily 8am–10pm in summer), a Venetian fortress built in 1557. There is a small museum of amphorae, and you can also clamber down into the prison cells, but the real attraction is the view over the rooftops and out to the Pakleni Islands and Vis on the horizon.

Hvar town Beaches

A short walk south from the ferry dock leads to a Franciscan monastery, on a headland overlooking a small pebble cove. On the far side of the harbour, the seafront promenade continues westwards for some 2km (1.2 miles), passing numerous rocky beaches and bathing platforms, popular with locals in summer.

For a lazy afternoon on the beach, a better option is to take a water-taxi to the **Pakleni Islands**, an emerald-green chain of islets just offshore from Hvar town, with pine woods and remote pebble beaches. The nearest island, **Jerolim**, is used by naturists; if you want to keep your clothes on, head for the largest island, **Sveti Kliment**.

Stari Grad

Until the Venetians moved the capital to Hvar town in the 13th century, this was the largest settlement on Hvar, founded by Greek settlers from Paros in the 4th century BC and named Pharos (from which Hvar is derived). Its current name, Stari Grad, simply means 'old town'. Although not as chic as Hvar town, this is nevertheless an attractive town, in a sheltered bay beside the island's chief ferry port.

The narrow cobbled streets behind the harbour are great for strolling, stumbling across hidden gems like the 12th-century **Chapel of St John**, with its 6th-century mosaics set into the floor. Near here is the archaeological site of Greek Pharos, where excavations are still going on.

Just back from the seafront, the **Tvrdalj Petra Hektorovića** (daily 10–1, 5–8, in summer) was the summer home of the poet Petar Hektorovic (1487–1572), designed as a fortress where the townspeople could take refuge in the event of a Turkish invasion. The walled garden with its fishpond and

Picture-perfect Pakleni Islands at sunset

pomegranate trees makes a good place to sit and contemplate the thoughtful Latin inscriptions with which the poet adorned his home – such as the skull and crossbones with the morbid reminder 'Neither riches nor fame, beauty nor age can save you from death'.

Jelsa

Hvar's third town, Jelsa, is on the north coast, looking across towards Brač and the Makarska Rivijera. In summer, this is undeniably a holiday town, with cafés on the promenade and rocky beaches backed by pine woods and hotels.

The one real sight is the 16th-century octagonal **Chapel of St John**, in a narrow lane behind the port. A 4km (2.5-mile) coastal path leads to the fishing village of Vrboska, a laid-back resort with some good beaches on the Glavica peninsula.

Water-taxis make the trip from Jelsa to Vrboska in summer, and to the islet of Zečevo, with its naturist beaches. If you feel like a change of scene, there are also excursion boats in the harbour offering day-trips to the famous Zlatni Rat beach on Brač (➤ 127).

Hvar's cathedral and main square

TAKING A BREAK

The harbourside in Hvar town seems to be one endless promenade in summer, and most visitors spend hours just sitting at waterfront cafés and bars watching life go by and looking out for celebrities on their yachts. **Ulica Petra Hektorovića**, one flight up towards the castle on the north side of the main square, is Hvar's trendy restaurant quarter, with a choice of three classy establishments on the same street (➤ 138–139).

➕ 199 E2

Tourist Information Office
✉ Trg Svetog Stjepana ☎ 021 741059; www.hvar.hr

HVAR: INSIDE INFO

Top tip There are **long waits for car ferries** to and from Hvar in summer, so plan your journey carefully and arrive at the harbour in plenty of time.

In more depth The pebble **beaches and coves of the south coast** are much less developed than those in Hvar town, Jelsa and Stari Grad. Get there by taking the road tunnel beneath the island's highest mountain, Sveti Nikola. The 8km (5-mile) stretch between Sveta Nedjelja and Zavala features isolated beaches and stone villages nestling beneath steep hillsides planted with south-facing vineyards, where much of Hvar's best wine is produced.

At Your Leisure

6 Nin

Crossing the stone bridge and walking through the entrance gate of this single-street town, built on an island in the lagoon at Dalmatia's northern tip, you would never guess that this was once the ecclesiastical and royal capital of Croatia. Between the 9th and 12th centuries, seven kings were crowned here and the bishop of Nin was the most powerful religious figure in the land. One famous bishop, Gregory of Nin, was immortalized in bronze by Ivan Meštrović; the original sculpture is in Split (▶ 125), but a copy is on display in Nin.

The greatest treasure of Nin is the 9th-century Church of the Holy Cross, a simple, whitewashed, domed chapel in the form of a Greek cross, which is sometimes claimed as the world's smallest cathedral. It stands all alone in a grassy field in the middle of town, surrounded by the ruins of a Roman temple.

Almost as spectacular is the Church of St Nicholas, built on a small burial mound 1km (half a mile) out of Nin on the road to Zadar; also dating from the 9th century, it is topped by a 16th-century tower added by the Venetians during their battles with the Turks. Sabunike, 2km (1.2 miles) north of Nin, has one of the finest sandy beaches in Croatia, with views to the island of Pag and the Velebit massif across the water.

✚ 198 B4
Tourist Information Office
✉ Trg Braće Radića 3 ☎ 023 265247

7 Zadar

The second largest city in Dalmatia was previously the Byzantine and Venetian capital and a naval power to rival Venice itself. These days, it is a strange mix of sprawling suburbs and a compact old town squeezed onto a narrow peninsula still partly enclosed by its medieval walls. Largely destroyed by Allied bombs during World War II, the old town has been heavily modernized, with the result that brutal concrete architecture and shopping arcades are found side by side with ancient churches and cobbled streets.

At the heart of it all is the old Roman Forum, whose stone was used in St Donat's Church, a lovely 9th-century Byzantine round church dedicated to an Irish bishop of Zadar who is said to have built it himself. Next to the church is the 12th-century Romanesque cathedral; you can climb the bell tower for stunning views. Also on the Forum is the church and convent of St Mary, whose treasury contains an exhibition of religious art entitled *Zlato i Srebro Zadra* (Gold and Silver of Zadar), with extravagant ornamental reliquaries produced by the city's gold and silversmiths (Mon–Sat 10–noon, 6–8, Apr–Sep; Mon–Sat 10–noon, 5–6.30, Oct–Mar).

For Kids
- Boat trips in the Nacionalni Park Krka (▶ 118–119)
- The natural history museum and zoo at Split (▶ 124)
- Bunari: Secrets of Šibenik is a themed multimedia exhibition on the history of Šibenik, in the vaults of the 15th-century wells beside the cathedral (daily 10am–11pm) (▶ 134)
- The beaches of the Makarska Rivijera (▶ 136)

The easiest approach to the old town is over the slender modern footbridge, though you can also enter via the Land Gate, a 16th-century triumphal arch topped by a Venetian winged lion and a macabre row of cattle skulls. Ferries leave from Zadar for the peaceful, unspoiled islands of Ugljan, Pašman and Dugi Otok (Long Island).

✚ 198 B4
Tourist Information Office
✉ Narodni Trg 5 ☎ 023 316166

8 Vransko Jezero

Croatia's largest natural lake is 25km (15.5 miles) south of Zadar, just inland from the beach resorts of Biograd and Pakoštane. Since 1999, the entire lake has been designated a nature park, attracting more than 100 species of waterfowl in winter and a colony of purple herons to the ornithological reserve on its north-west shore. In summer, you can rent rowing boats to go out on the lake, or follow the 30km (18-mile) cycle trail around its shore.

✚ 198 C4

9 Nacionalni Park Kornati

A cruise through the Kornati Islands is unforgettable. Off the coast between Zadar and Šibenik, this is an ethereal seascape of cliffs, coves, underwater caves and rocky islets, described by the Irish playwright George Bernard Shaw (1856–1950) as having been created by the gods out of the stars and their own tears.

The Kornati National Park contains 89 islands and reefs, but the archipelago has over 140, stretching north as far as the spectacular Telašćica Bay on Dugi Otok. For most of the year, the islands are uninhabited, but in summer the residents of Murter set up fish restaurants in the bays and rent out stone cottages and fishing boats for a 'Robinson Crusoe' experience. The islands are a paradise for sailors and the best way to see them is undoubtedly on your own yacht, though tour operators also offer day excursions from Murter, Zadar and Šibenik.

✚ 198 B3
Tourist Information Office
✉ Ulica Butina 2, Murter ☎ 022 434662/435740; www.kornati.hr
🎟 Park: expensive

10 Šibenik Cathedral

The 15th-century Cathedral of St James, standing proud above the mouth of the River Krka, is perhaps the finest example of church architecture in Croatia. It is mostly the work of Juraj Dalmatinac (George the Dalmatian), a Zadar-born architect who trained in Venice; a sculpture of him by Ivan Meštrović stands on the cathedral square. After his death in 1473, the work was completed by Nikola Firentinac (Nicholas of Florence), who added the dome and the distinctive barrel-vaulted roof. The result is a harmonious blend of Venetian Gothic and Renaissance styles. The outer portals, sculpted by Dalmatinac, are full of florid detail. The side door, facing the town hall, is flanked by a pair of roaring lions and statues of Adam and Eve, each with one hand on their heart and the other protecting their modesty.

Near here is Dalmatinac's playful masterpiece, the frieze of 74 stone heads running

The islands of Kornati National Park are best seen by boat

around the exterior of the apses, depicting a fascinating cross-section of 15th-century society; they are said to be portraits of those citizens who refused to pay towards the cost of the cathedral. Inside the building, don't miss the tiny hidden baptistery, reached down a flight of steps to the right of the altar, with delicately carved stone angels beneath a vaulted roof.

🔢 198 C3 ✉ Trg Republike Hrvatske, Šibenik 🕐 Daily 9–7 💷 Free

The cathedral of St James at Šibenik

🔟 Salona

The most significant archaeological site in Croatia is also a highly atmospheric place, the ruins of a Roman city of 60,000 people surrounded by fields with the tower blocks of Split visible just below. In Roman times, this was the largest town on the coast, flourishing from the 2nd century BC to the 5th century AD; the emperor Diocletian is thought to have been born here.

Just inside the entrance gate, the necropolis of Manastirine has the feel of an archaeological junk shop, with tombs and sarcophagi scattered among piles of stones. In the presbytery of a Roman basilica is the vaulted tomb of Domnius, the first bishop of Salona, executed in the nearby amphitheatre in AD 304

Salona's Roman amphitheatre

during Diocletian's persecution of Christians.

From the Tusculum archaeological museum, a path leads to the lower town, based around the ruins of an impressive church. You can walk along the Roman walls and into the fields to reach the well-preserved amphitheatre, with seating for 15,000 spectators. Many of the treasures from Salona are now on display in the Archaeological Museum at Split (► 125).

🔢 199 D3 ✉ 5km (3 miles) from Split
☎ 021 212900 🚌 Bus from Split
🕐 Mon–Fri 7–7, Sat 10–7, Sun 4–7 in summer; daily 9–3 in winter
💷 Inexpensive

🔢 Vis

One of Croatia's remotest inhabited islands was closed to foreigners from World War II until 1989, when it was used by the Yugoslav army as a military base. Apart from a few fishermen and winemakers, most of the islanders left during that time, but Vis is now reaping the benefit as, spared the impact of mass tourism, it is fast developing a reputation as a fashionable resort. Expensive yachts are moored in the harbour in

Castles in the Air

Inland from the Dalmatian coast are two historic fortresses whose fortunes mirror the region's history. In the 10th century, both were strongholds for the medieval Croatian kings, while in the 16th century, they were occupied by the Turks, becoming key strategic bases on the borders of the Venetian and Ottoman empires. The castle at Klis (daily 9–7, in summer; 10–4, in winter) sits on a rocky bluff just inland from Salona; you can climb its grassy ramparts for wonderful views. The fortress at Knin (Tue–Sun 9–5), 56km (35 miles) inland from Šibenik, was occupied in the 1990s by troops of the Republic of the Serbian Krajina, based at Knin; the Croatian flag now flies symbolically from the battlements following its liberation in 1995 in the final act of the Homeland War.

summer, and the island can now be reached by daily catamaran from Split in under two hours.

It was the Greeks who founded the settlement of Issa, on the site of present-day Vis town in the 4th century BC; the remains of an ancient Greek cemetery lie just back from the harbour. During the Napoleonic wars (1811–15), the island was occupied by the British, who also had a base here during World War II, when Tito briefly set up his head-quarters in a cave on Mount Hum. Walk onto the cliffs on the west side of the harbour to reach the abandoned George III fortress, with a crudely carved Union Jack (British flag) above the door and superb views over the bay towards Hvar.

On the far side of the bay, a stroll through the suburb of Kut leads to a small English cemetery, with memorials to victims of the Napoleonic wars and the 'comrades of Tito's liberation war'. Buses from Vis town make the journey across the island, passing vineyards and steep terraces on the way to the attractive fishing port of Komiža. Boats depart from Komiža in summer for excursions into the Modra Špilja (Blue Cave), a natural wonder on the nearby island of Biševo.

🔴 199 D2
Tourist Information Office
✉ Šetalište Stare Isse 5
☎ 021 711144

🔟 Makarska

The string of pebble beaches in the shadow of the Biokovo massif is known as the Makarska Rivijera. Former fishing villages such as Brela, Baška Voda, Tučepi and Podgora are now attractive summer resorts, while the town of Makarska, set in a horse-shoe bay, gets very lively in high season. This is where package tourism has made the greatest impact in Dalmatia, and Makarska certainly lacks the character and charm of some of the Venetian towns on this coast, though it makes a good base for a relaxed family holiday.

Looming over the coast is the table mountain of Biokovo, whose summit, Sveti Jure (1,762m/5,781 feet), is the second highest in Croatia. Climb to Sveti Jure from Makarska for views stretching all the way to Italy on a clear day.

🔴 199 F2
Tourist Information Office
✉ Obala Kralja Tomislava
☎ 021 612002

Beaches along the Makarska riviera below the Biokovo massif

Where to... Stay

Prices
Expect to pay per person per night for a double room
€ under 250kn   €€ 250kn–500kn   €€€ over 500kn

BRAČ

Kaštil €€

If you want to be in town rather than by the beach, stay in this old stone building beside the harbour. All of the rooms have sea views and some have balconies; the restaurant is on a terrace above the sea.

➕ 199 E2 🗺 Ulica Frane Radića 1, Bol ☎ 021 635995; www.kastil.hr
🕑 Mar–Oct

HVAR

Palace €€€

This is the place to stay in Hvar if you want to do it in style. The Palace is built on the site of the old Venetian governor's palace, incorporating the clock tower and loggia in its façade. In summer, you can have a drink on the first-floor terrace overlooking the harbour; in winter, you can swim in a heated seawater pool. For something a little less swanky, try the Slavija (under the same ownership), in an old stone building on the promenade.

➕ 199 E2 🗺 Trg Svetog Stjepana, Hvar town ☎ 021 741966;
www.suncanihvar.hr

NACIONALI PARK KRKA

Skradinski Buk €€

Most people visit the waterfalls as a day-trip from the coast, but to explore the national park in depth, stay at this family-run hotel, which opened in 2002 in a restored town house in the waterfront village of Skradin. The 28 rooms are simply furnished and painted in warm pastel shades, and the third-floor terrace has river views. The ferry dock for the national park shuttle boats is 300m (330 yards) away.

➕ 198 C3 🗺 Burinovac, Skradin
☎ 022 771771; www.skradinskibuk.hr

SPLIT

Jadran €€

Jadran is a stylish, modern hotel on the seafront, just beyond the marina, a 20-minute walk from central Split. Most of the 30 rooms look out over the sea or the gardens of Sustipan Park. The hotel has its own Olympic-sized swimming pool, tennis courts and a fitness centre.

➕ 199 D3 🗺 Sustipanski Put 23
☎ 021 398622; www.hoteljadran.hr

TROGIR

Concordia €€

This 18th-century town house near the Kamerlengo fortress is now a small hotel, with views across to the island of Čiovo. Each of the 14 rooms has a shower, TV and air-conditioning. An added bonus is the reserved parking space for hotel guests.

➕ 199 D3 🗺 Obala Bana Berislavića 22 ☎ 021 885400;
www.concordia-hotel.htnet.hr

VIS

Tamaris €

Occupying a 19th-century Habsburg villa in the heart of Vis town, Tamaris is a short walk from the ferry port. The 27 rooms have high ceilings and wooden floors. Ask for a room overlooking the harbour as there are lovely views across the bay.

➕ 199 D2 🗺 Obala Sveti Jurja 20, Vis town ☎ 021 711350

Where to...
Eat and Drink

Prices
Expect to pay for a three-course meal for one, excluding drinks and service

€ under 100kn €€ 100k–150kn €€€ over 150kn

BRAČ

Konoba Marija €€

This must have the most perfect setting of just about any restaurant in Croatia – high up on a terrace, gazing across the pine woods to the island of Hvar across the sea. You can get there by walking or cycling the 4km (2.5-mile) dirt track from Bol along the cliffs to the wine village of Murvica; it is also possible to drive here. Meat and fish are barbecued on an open grill – try the Brač lamb or the mixed grill for two, perhaps accompanied by a jug of wine from the local vineyards.

A nice touch is the basket of garlic bread, toasted on the grill and brought to the table with your meal.

⊞ 199 E2 ⊠ Murvica, near Bol ☎ 091 524 7439 Ⓢ Daily 10am–midnight, Apr–Oct

Palute €€

Popular Palut is right on the waterfront in Supetar, close to the dock where the ferries arrive from Split. It serves a full range of grilled meat and fish dishes at reasonable prices. Come here for good, simple, local food – try the Brač sheep's cheese followed by grilled lamb with chips and salad. The same family owns a comfortable bed-and-breakfast a short walk from the port.

⊞ 199 E3 ⊠ Porat 4, Supeta ☎ 021 631730 Ⓢ Daily 10am–midnight, Apr–Oct

HVAR

Konoba Menego €€

Dine by candlelight or eat outside, with a wine barrel for a table, at this family-run tavern in an old stone house on the steps leading up from the harbour to the castle. Everything here is home-made or produced locally, from the Pakleni Islands wine to the Hvar goat's cheese with honey. Much of the menu consists of plates of cold meats and cheeses, so it's ideal for snacking rather than a full meal. For pudding, try the 'drunken figs', stuffed with almonds and soaked in brandy, followed by Turkish coffee with walnut or wild orange liqueur. The Kovačević family also own a vineyard and summer restaurant on the nearby island of Sveti Kliment.

⊞ 199 E2 ⊠ Groda, Hvar town ☎ 021 742036 Ⓢ Daily noon–2, 5–10, Apr–Oct

Luna €€

Luna is one of a trio of trendy restaurants along the same street, just a flight of steps up from the main square. This chic trattoria features Italian and Mediterranean cuisine, from fresh pasta dishes and steak with truffles to gazpacho, salads and fish stew with potatoes and white wine. On warm evenings you can dine on the roof terrace.

⊞ 199 E2 ⊠ Ulica Petra Hektorovića 5, Hvar town ☎ 021 741400 Ⓢ Daily noon–midnight, Apr–Oct

Paladini €€€

This elegant restaurant is housed in a lovely 16th-century Renaissance palace, once given to the noble Paladini family as reward for service in a sea battle between the Venetian and Turkish fleets. It serves

Dalmatian cuisine, fresh fish, grilled squid and pasta dishes, served in a garden of orange and lemon trees.

🚩 199 E2 ✉ Ulica Petra Hektorovića 4, Hvar town ☎ 021 742104 🕐 Daily noon–3, 6–midnight, Apr–Oct

Zlatna Školjka €€€

In Hvar's trendy restaurant quarter, the 'golden shell' advertises 'slow food', using local ingredients and inventive takes on traditional dishes, such as goat's cheese in olive oil, gnocchi with almonds, beef stuffed with goat's cheese or rabbit with figs. Booking advised, especially in July and August.

🚩 199 E2 ✉ Ulica Petra Hektorovića 8, Hvar town ☎ 098 168 8797 🕐 Daily noon–3, 7–midnight, in summer

SPLIT

Kod Jože €€€

Hidden away in an old stone house on a quiet lane near Strossmayerov Park, this excellent *konoba* (tavern) serves first-class meat and fish dishes. The fresh fish and seafood can be pricey, but there is a range of less expensive grills and pizzas, as well as traditional Dalmatian dishes such as *muškalica* (beef stewed with onions and white wine).

🚩 199 D3 ✉ Obrov 1 ☎ 021 884811 🕐 Daily noon–11

TROGIR

Fontana €€

The back streets of Trogir offer a wide choice of restaurants, many with attractive courtyards and summer gardens, but for waterfront dining the best option is the seafront terrace of this town-house hotel, just back from the Riva

🚩 199 D3 ✉ Ulica Sredmanuška 4 ☎ 021 347397 🕐 Daily 9am–11pm

VIS

Doručak Kod Tihane €€€

The first tourist hotel in Vis, dating from 1911, reopened its doors in 2004 as a smart waterfront restaurant, whose name means 'Breakfast at Tiffany's'. The original art nouveau interior has been carefully restored, with chandeliers and exposed stone walls. On summer nights, you can dine on the terrace, with candlelight and dreamy views across the water adding to the romantic atmosphere. The emphasis in the restaurant is on seafood, with fish pâté, shrimp risotto, grilled squid, sautéed mussels and grilled fresh fish featuring on the menu, best washed down with the local Vugava wine. Finish your meal with a plate of *hruštule* – traditional pastries from Vis.

🚩 199 D2 ✉ Obala Sveti Jurja 5, Vis town ☎ 021 718472 🕐 Daily 9–2, 6–midnight

Villa Kaliopa €€€

During the summer months, the harbour at Vis fills up with yachts, many of whose owners dine in this exclusive and romantic restaurant, with fountains and statues in the walled garden of a 16th-century villa. The menu focuses on fresh fish and seafood and changes according to what is in available locally in the market, but the waiter will recommend the best dishes of the day. If you need to ask the prices, you probably can't afford to eat here.

🚩 199 D2 ✉ Ulica Vladimira Nazora 32, Vis town ☎ 021 711755 🕐 Daily noon–3, 5–midnight, in summer

Where to... Shop

The best shopping areas are in the towns of Split, Šibenik, Trogir and Zadar. Trendy Hvar town has a number of fashionable and offbeat boutiques. Each of the islands has its own speciality – lavender in Hvar, marble in Brač, wine in Vis.

HVAR AND VIS

Wherever you go on Hvar in summer, you will find street stalls offering **lavender** in numerous forms – dried flowers, oil, soap and shampoo.

Another unusual souvenir of Hvar is **lace** made out of the agave plant; it is produced exclusively by the nuns of the Benedictine convent in Hvar town, using a technique imported from the Canary Islands.

In both Hvar and Vis, you will come across wine-cellars selling the local wine. On Vis, look out for the delicious dry white Vugava and the red Viški Plavac.

SPLIT

Croatia's second city has a full range of department stores, shopping malls and boutiques. Most of the shopping is concentrated in the busy pedestrian streets of the medieval town, set just back from the waterfront. The main thoroughfare is **Marmontova**, where several trendy boutiques sell women's fashions and shoes, including imported Italian designer brands at reasonable prices. The stalls in the underground galleries of **Diocletian's Palace** sell a mixture of arts and crafts and cheap tourist souvenirs.

Split's main market, **Pazar**, is outside the eastern gate of the palace; this is where you will find everything from organic grapes to cheap trainers.

Where to... Be Entertained

Entertainment on the Dalmatian islands and coast takes many forms, from windsurfing, scuba diving and river-rafting to drinking at waterfront bars.

MUSIC AND DRAMA

Most towns on the coast organize some sort of cultural festival in summer, with concerts and performances in local churches and open-air venues in July and August. Among the events to look out for are recitals of medieval, baroque and chamber music in **St Donat's Church in Zadar**, and concerts in **Trogir cathedral** and the courtyard of the **Kamerlengo fortress**.

In Split, performances of opera, ballet and drama take place throughout the year at the **Hrvatsko Narodno Kazalište** (Croatian National Theatre) on Trg Gaje Bulata (tel: 021 363014; www.hnk-split.hr), but the big event is the **Split Summer Festival**. For four weeks in July and August, the peristyle of Diocletian's Palace becomes an open-air stage; the highlight is the performance of Verdi's opera *Aida*.

In Hvar town, try to take in a performance at the **Hvarsko Kazalište**, which opened in 1612, although extensively restored in the 19th century, it retains much of its original feel, with plush red seats and a painted ceiling. Performances of classical and modern drama take place throughout the summer, when there are also evening concerts in the nearby Franciscan monastery.

Dubrovnik and South Dalmatia

Getting Your Bearings

The southern Dalmatian coastline is dominated by Dubrovnik, a perfectly preserved walled city described by the English poet Lord Byron (1788–1824) as the 'pearl of the Adriatic'.

While much of Dalmatia was controlled by Venice, for 450 years Dubrovnik was the powerful city-state of Ragusa, paying notional tribute to Ottoman sultans and Hungarian kings, but refusing to be ruled by either. During its golden age in the 15th and 16th centuries, the city grew rich on

shipping and was known as the 'Croatian Athens', a melting-pot of cultures and a meeting-place for the greatest artists, scientists, cartographers and sailors of the day. It was during this time that the city walls were built, and a walk around the walls still provides one of the most memorable experiences of a visit to Croatia.

After suffering extensive damage during the siege of 1991–2, Dubrovnik has been brilliantly restored and once again has the feel of a lively open-air museum, with churches, palaces, cafés and flagstoned streets.

Dubrovnik makes a good base for visiting the rest of southern Dalmatia, from the unspoiled islands of Mljet, Lopud and

Rose window in the Franciscan monastery

Above: the city walls of Dubrovnik

Šipan to the vineyards of the Pelješac peninsula and the mini-Dubrovnik of Korčula town. North of Dubrovnik, the Magistrala coastal highway passes through a short section of Bosnia-Hercegovina (passports required) on its way to the Neretva delta, where many of Croatia's citrus fruits are grown. To the south, beyond the pretty resort of Cavtat, the fertile Konavle Valley is squeezed between the mountains of Bosnia and Montenegro.

Right: boats moored to the jetty at Cavtat

★ Don't Miss

At Your Leisure

Tending the grape vines

There is more to southern Dalmatia than Dubrovnik. Walk through woodland gardens, sample Croatia's most famous wine and visit a remote island monastery on this brief introduction to the highlights of the region.

Dubrovnik and South Dalmatia in Three Days

Day One

Morning
Take your time exploring the old town of **❶ Dubrovnik** (left, ➤ 146–149), soaking up the atmosphere in its streets and squares. A good way to take the pulse of the city is to walk in the steep lanes and historic districts which rise to either side of the main thoroughfare, Stradun. Afterwards, relax with a coffee on the terrace of Gradska Kavana before a seafood lunch by the harbour at Lokanda Peskarija (➤ 160).

Afternoon and Evening
Take a stroll around Dubrovnik's city walls, gazing down over the rooftops and out to sea. The ticket for the walls also gives access to Tvrđava Lovrijenac, outside the Pile Gate. Climb the steps to the fortress for wonderful sunset views, then have dinner at Orhan (➤ 160), overlooking a peaceful cove in the shadow of the fort.

Day Two
Morning and Afternoon
Go down to the harbour at Gruž to catch the *Nona Ana* catamaran, which

leaves at 9am daily in summer for **2 Mljet** (right, ➤ 150–151). This gives you six hours on the island, enough time to explore the Mljet National Park on foot and by bicycle and take a boat to Benediktinski Samostan St Mary's, a monastery on an islet in the middle of a lake.

Evening

Spend your second evening in Dubrovnik inside the old city, which gets particularly animated on summer nights. If you can, take in a performance during the Summer Festival (➤ 162); otherwise, have dinner at Rozarij (➤ 160) then head to the Troubadour café, which has live jazz at around 10pm most nights.

Day Three

Morning

Head north along the Magistrala coast road, pausing to walk around the gardens at **6 Trsteno** (➤ 156) before continuing to the **5 Pelješac** peninsula (➤ 155). After a lunch of local oysters beside the harbour at Mali Ston, you can walk off your meal with a circuit of the walls at nearby Veli Ston.

Afternoon and Evening

Drive across the Pelješac Peninsula, perhaps stopping to taste and buy wine at the Dingač vineyards in Potomje. Arrive at Orebić in time to make the short ferry crossing to **3 Korčula** (below, ➤ 152–154). Spend the evening walking around Korčula town and having dinner on the sea walls at **Morski Konjic** (➤ 161). On Monday and Thursday nights in summer, you can catch a performance of *moreška* sword dances (➤ 26–27) beside the Revelin tower.

◯ Dubrovnik Old Town

Dubrovnik is the jewel in Croatia's crown – a beautifully restored city, full of Gothic and Renaissance architecture, crowded onto a rocky headland and surrounded by its 15th-century walls.

From 1358 to 1808, this was the republic of Ragusa, one of the wealthiest cities in Europe, whose merchant fleet was reputed to be the third largest in the world. Much of the city was rebuilt following an earthquake in 1667, but although many fine buildings were destroyed, what remains has a harmonious feel.

Dubrovnik came to the world's attention during the siege of 1991–2, when Serb shells fell on the old city and over 70 per cent of houses were hit. Walking around Dubrovnik today, there are few signs of the recent war and the maps at the entrance gates, pinpointing the damage in detail, come as quite a shock. The city has recovered its confidence, the tourists have returned and there is a buzz about the outdoor cafés once again.

The ravages of war are no longer evident in Dubrovnik old town

Getting There

Cars are not allowed inside the walls and the old city is eminently walkable. The best entrance is through the **Vrata od Pile** (Pile Gate), where most local buses stop. Cross the stone bridge and wooden drawbridge to reach the outer gate. Above the archway is a figure of St Blaise, a 3rd-century bishop from Armenia who was martyred by the Romans and became the patron saint of Dubrovnik after he appeared in a dream to a local priest, warning of a Venetian attack. The Pile Gate leads straight into Stradun, the old city's main street. The other main entrance is the **Vrata od Ploče** (Ploče Gate), at the eastern end of the city close to some of Dubrovnik's best hotels.

Looking down the Stradun, Dubrovnik's best-known shopping street

Stradun

The best-known avenue in Croatia is both a busy shopping street and the venue for the *korzo* or nightly promenade. Once lined with palaces, it was rebuilt after the earthquake in uniform style, its houses and shopfronts each having arched doorways at ground level and green-shuttered window-frames above.

At the east end, beneath the clock tower, Stradun broadens out into Luža Square, with the **Orlando column** (➤ 178) in the middle. On one side is the **Church of Sv. Vlaha**, with an altar containing a 15th-century gilded statue of the saint; on the other is the **Sponza** palace, Ragusa's former customs house and a rare survivor of the earthquake. It now houses the city archives and a memorial room to the defenders of Dubrovnik who held fast during the 1991–2 siege.

Franjevački Samostan

Just inside the Pile Gate, this church contains a beautiful 14th-century cloister. The museum includes a 15th-century wooden portrait of St Blaise and a painting of pre-earthquake Dubrovnik. Also off the cloister is a dispensary dating from 1317, said to be the oldest continuously operating pharmacy in Europe.

A Walk Around the Walls

The high point of any visit to Dubrovnik is a walk around the city walls, up to 25m (82 feet) high and 6m (19 feet) thick in places, reinforced with bastions and towers. The complete circuit is about 2km (1.2 miles) and takes at least an hour, looking down over courtyards, gardens and restored rooftops, as well as giving superb views out to sea and the isle of Lokrum offshore. For the finest views, climb to the roof of the Tvrđava Minčeta, designed by the Florentine Michelozzo Michelozzi in 1455. The best place to begin a circuit of the walls is just inside the Pile Gate, though there is also access from Ploče Gate and Tvrđava Sv. Ivana. The walls are open daily from 9–7 in summer and 9–3 in winter and the entrance fee is used to fund restoration projects. The ticket is also valid for Fort Lovrijenac, a free-standing fortress outside the Pile Gate.

Dominikanski Samostan

This 15th-century church is reached by a grand staircase inside the Ploče Gate. The highlight is the delightful cloister of orange trees. The museum contains a painting of Mary Magdalene by Titian (c1488–1576), and the church features a Virgin and Child by Ivan Meštrović (1883–1962).

Above: the
Rector's Palace
is now the city
museum

Katedrala

Dubrovnik's baroque cathedral was completed in 1713, replacing an earlier church destroyed in the earthquake. The white walls give it a feeling of light and space, in contrast to the treasury behind the altar. This macabre collection features rich gold and silver filigree work, designed by local artists. Among the items on display is a skull case for the head of St Blaise, and a 16th-century casket said to contain Jesus's nappy.

Above left:
rooftop view of
the old city

The cloisters in the Franciscan monastery

Kneževe Dvor

Dubrovnik's city museum occupies the Rector's Palace, the former seat of the Ragusan republic where the *knez* (rector) would spend his entire term of office of just one month. The exhibits include the the state apartments filled with period furniture and the former dungeons. During the Summer Festival, classical concerts are held in the courtyard.

➕ 202 A2
Tourist Information Office
✉ Stradun ☎ 020 321561; www.tzdubrovnik.hr

Franjevački Samostan
➕ 202 A2 ✉ Stradun 2 ⏱ Daily 9–6 💵 Inexpensive

Dominikanski Samostan
➕ 202 B2 ✉ Ulica Svetog Dominika ⏱ Daily 9–6, in summer; 9–3 in winter 💵 Inexpensive

Katedrala
➕ 202 B1 ✉ Pred Dvorom ⏱ Mon–Sat 8–8, Sun 11–5, in summer; Mon–Sat 8–5, Sun 11–5, in winter. Treasury Mon–Sat 8–5.30, Sun 11–5, all year 💵 Treasury: inexpensive

Kneževe Dvor
➕ 202 B1 ✉ Pred Dvorom ⏱ Daily 9–6, Jun–Sep; Mon–Sat 9–2, rest of year 💵 Moderate

DUBROVNIK OLD TOWN: INSIDE INFO

Top tips The tourist office on Stradun has free copies of the **monthly Dubrovnik Guide**, with museum and event listings, bus maps and timetables.
• Dubrovnik's **city beach** is at Banje, outside the Ploče Gate, a broad sweep of pebble beach with views to the old town.

Hidden gem The **Sinagoga** (Synagogue) on Ulica Žudioska serves Dubrovnik's small Jewish community, one of the earliest Sephardic congregations in the world, following their expulsion from Spain in 1492. Among the items on display in the museum is a list of earthquake victims from 1667 and a memorial to 27 Dubrovnik Jews who died during the Holocaust.

② Mljet

The southernmost of Croatia's major islands is a beautiful and unspoiled place of pine and oak forests, steep cliffs, saltwater lakes and coves.

Mljet is 37km (23 miles) long and just 3km (2 miles) wide. It has a mythical appeal for Croatians, as the legendary home of the nymph Calypso, who is said to have seduced Ulysses and held him captive for seven years in her cave on the south coast after he was shipwrecked on the island. The story is told by Homer in his epic poem *Odyssey*.

Most people come here on day-trips to visit the **Nacionalni Park Mljet** (Mljet National Park), which covers 31sq km (12 sq miles) of forest and lakes on the west of the island. The easiest way to get there is on the daily catamaran *Nona Ana*, which makes the journey from Dubrovnik in under two hours. Tickets go on sale at 8am each morning in the kiosk opposite the quayside at Gruž. From June to September, the boat takes you to **Polače**, inside the national park, allowing you six hours on the island; at other times, when the boat drops you at Sobra, you will probably need an overnight stay. In summer, you can also visit Mljet on organized excursions from Dubrovnik, Cavtat, Korčula and Orebić, with entry to the national park included in the price.

Much of Mljet Island is now a national park

Did You Know?

Mljet is the only place in Europe to be home to wild mongooses. The Indian grey mongoose was introduced here in 1910 in an attempt to rid the island of snakes and it has now become established.

Arriving at **Polače**, you can buy a ticket and pick up a map from the kiosk by the harbour. The ticket includes a minibus transfer to the park headquarters at Pristanište, but it is just as pleasant to walk on the well-marked path beginning behind the ruins of a 4th-century Roman palace. This brings you out by the shore of Veliko Jezero, the larger of two salt-water lakes connected to the sea by a narrow channel. A foot-path leads around the two lakes, which meet at Stari Most (Old Bridge), where you can rent bicycles, canoes and rowing boats in summer.

The ticket also includes a boat transfer from Pristanište or Stari Most to **St Mary's Island**, where you will find one of Croatia's most photographed sights – a 12th-century Benedictine monastery, on an islet in the middle of the lake. Used as a hotel during the Yugoslav era, the monastery is now in a poor state of repair, but it is still an atmospheric place.

A distant view of the island of Mljet

TAKING A BREAK

There are several cafés and restaurants on the **seafront at Polače**, a summer restaurant on **St Mary's Island**, and another, **Mali Raj**, on the shores of Veliko Jezero.

➕ 198 A1

Nacionalni Park Mljet
✉ Pristanište 2 ☎ 020 744058; www.np-mljet.hr 💷 Expensive

MLJET: INSIDE INFO

Top tip Climb to the summit of **Montokuc** (253m/830 feet), the highest point in the national park, for views across the island. The path is signposted from the shores of Veliko Jezero, near Pristanište.

In more depth Although most people visit on day-trips, it is possible to stay on the island. There is a hotel at Pomena (➤ 159), and several places offer rooms on the waterfront at Polače. Saplunara, on the southern tip of Mljet, has one of Dalmatia's finest sandy beaches; although the village is almost deserted, local families rent out rooms here and set up fish restaurants in summer.

3 Korčula

The Venetian walled town of Korčula is like a miniature version of Dubrovnik, standing proud on its own peninsula, with the sea on three sides. It lies on the edge of one of the greenest islands in the Adriatic, with cypress and pine forests and vineyards planted by the ancient Greeks.

The easiest way of getting to Korčula from southern Dalmatia is on the regular ferries from Orebić on the Pelješac peninsula. The car ferry arrives at **Dominče**, 2km (1.2 miles) south of Korčula town; if you are touring without a car, there is a passenger ferry which docks right on the harbour at Korčula.

A passenger ferry moored at Korčula harbour

The main coastal ferry from Rijeka to Dubrovnik calls in at Korčula, and there are also ferries and catamarans from Split to Vela Luka, the island's main town, 45km (28 miles) from Korčula at its western tip. Another alternative in summer is a ferry to Dominče from Drvenik on the Makarska Rivijera.

The Town

Korčula is a compact town, huddled onto a narrow peninsula and still largely enclosed by its medieval walls and round towers. The old town is perfect for walking, and the stroll around the outer walls on a pine-shaded promenade takes all of 15 minutes. From here there are views to the mountains of the Pelješac Peninsula, just 2km (1.2 miles) away.

The main entry to the old town is through the **Kopnena Vrata** (Land Gate), reached by a broad flight of steps leading up to the Revelin Tower. Above the arch is a

relief of the winged lion of St Mark, the symbol of Venice. The 15th-century tower has been restored to house a permanent exhibition on the *moreška* sword dancers (► 26–27), who can be seen performing nearby twice a week in summer.

From here, a single street runs the length of the old town, with narrow lanes dropping down to the sea on either side. Almost immediately you reach the tiny main square, dominated by the **Cathedral of St Mark**, begun in the 13th century and completed over the next 300 years in a mix of Gothic and Renaissance styles.

Next door, the **Treasury** houses an eclectic collection of artworks, from a 15th-century altarpiece and some English alabaster sculptures of Christ's passion to drawings by Tiepolo and Raphael and a naïve *Annunciation* by local artist Ana Fištanic, depicting an angel in rainbow wings appearing to the Virgin dressed in Korčula peasant costume. The **Town Museum** (daily 9–1, 5–7, Jun–Sep; by prior appointment, Oct–May), in a 16th-century Renaissance palace, is just across the square.

Arriving by the old town's gated entrance

TAKING A BREAK
The **Gaudi cocktail bar** on Šetalište Petra Kanavelica makes a great place for a sunset apéritif on the sea walls.

➕ 199 F2

Tourist Information Office
✉ Obala Franje Tuđmana ☎ 020 715701

KORČULA: INSIDE INFO

Top tips Try to catch a performance of the **moreška sword dance**, which takes place at festivals and on Monday and Thursday evenings throughout the summer.
• Look out for the **white wines** produced on the island, not just Grk from Lumbarda but also Pošip and Rukatac.
• Take a water-taxi in summer to the **island of Badija**, which has several good pebble beaches including one naturist beach. Alternatively, take a bus or boat trip to the wine village of Lumbarda, 6km (4 miles) from Korčula, where you can walk through the vineyards to the beautiful sandy beach at Prižna.

Hidden gem The **Icon Museum** (daily 10–1, 6–8 in summer), in a narrow lane off Šetalište Petra Kanavelića, contains a collection of Cretan Orthodox icons, looted during a war between Venetian and Turkish troops. A covered bridge from the museum leads into All Saints' Church, with a carved wooden altarpiece sheltering beneath a 15th-century canopy.

At Your Leisure

4 Lastovo

This remote island south of Korčula was closed to foreigners from 1976 to 1989 and is still very much off the tourist trail, though it is fast developing as a chic destination for sailors and independent tourists. Once part of the Ragusan republic, it is now connected by ferry to Split rather than Dubrovnik, though you can also get there from Hvar and Vela Luka on Korčula. Ferries arrive at the port of Ubli, 10km (6 miles) from Lastovo town, the island's biggest village.

With a population of under 1,000, Lastovo feels like a place apart and there is little to do but walk in the fertile countryside, swim from secluded beaches and take boat trips in summer to the uninhabited islets of the archipelago. Like Istria, Lastovo was part of Italy between the two world wars and many older people speak Italian.

On Shrove Tuesday each year, the island plays host to one of Croatia's strangest Carnival celebrations, when a straw figure known as Poklad is paraded through town on a donkey before being ritually burned, while dancers perform a local variation of the Korčula sword dance.

🔲 199 F1
Tourist Information Office
✉ Lastovo town ☎ 020 801018

5 Pelješac

This long mountainous finger of land is effectively an island, known throughout Croatia for its expensive Dingač and Postup red wines. A single road runs the 90km (56 miles) length of the peninsula, with views across to the islands of Korčula, Lastovo, Mljet, Hvar and Vis.

The twin towns of Mali Ston and Ston guard the entrance to the peninsula, fortified by 14th-century walls

Vineyards on the Pelješac peninsula

Pelješac Wines

You can taste and buy local wines at the Dingač and Matuško Vina wineries in the village of Potomje. The best red wine, Dingač, is produced from Plavac Mali grapes grown on the southern sea-facing slopes.
Dingač (tel: 020 742010)
Matuško Vina (tel: 020 742393)

which once formed the second longest defensive system in the world, after the Great Wall of China. You can walk right around the walls at Ston; the section from here to Mali Ston is being restored. From Ston, the road passes through the vineyards at Potomje, the heart of production for Dingač wines, on its way to the pleasant beach resort of Orebić, 2km (1.2 miles) from Korčula across a narrow channel.

➕ 198 A2
Tourist Information Office
✉ Trg Mimbeli, Orebić
☎ 020 713718

6 Trsteno

The 16th-century aristocrat Ivan Gučetić built his summer villa in the seaside village of Trsteno, where leading poets, artists and statesmen of Ragusan society would gather to discuss politics and stroll in the elegant gardens overlooking the sea. The house and garden remained in the Gučetić family until 1947, when they were confiscated by the state.

Now an arboretum, the gardens make a lovely place to walk, with shady avenues, hedges and exotic trees, many grown from seeds brought back by local sailors from their travels. The highlight is the ornamental fishpond, just behind the villa, where a figure of Neptune with

The Grotto in the garden at Trsteno

his trident stands guard over a grotto, flanked by a pair of nymphs.

The gardens were badly damaged by fire caused by shelling in 1991, but fortunately they have recovered well. A steep path leads down to Trsteno's harbour, with views of the Elafiti Islands offshore.

➕ 198 B1 ☎ 020 751019 ⏲ Daily 8–8, in summer; 8–5, in winter
💲 Moderate

7 Elafitski Otoci (Elafiti Islands

The tiny, car-free islands of Koločep,

For Kids
• The walk around Dubrovnik's city walls (➤ 148)
• *Moreška* sword dances on Korčula (➤ 26–27 and 154)
• Swimming in the Dead Sea on Lokrum (➤ 157)
• The beaches around Cavtat (➤ 157)

Čilipi

Cavtat is the main town of the Konavle region, a narrow strip of land between Dubrovnik and the Montenegrin border. The area is known for the folk costumes of its inhabitants, which can be seen every Sunday morning in summer in the village of Čilipi, when folklore performances and traditional courtship dances are put on for tourists in front of the church.

Lopud and Šipan provide peaceful havens just a short ferry ride away from the bustle of Dubrovnik.

During the golden age of Ragusa, many Dubrovnik nobles built their summer houses here, and the islands are still a popular weekend retreat. There are regular ferries to the Elafiti Islands from the harbour at Gruž, with additional fast shuttle boats from Dubrovnik's old port in summer, making it possible to combine a trip to two of the islands in one day.

With orchards, vegetable gardens, vineyards, pine woods, ancient stone chapels and churches, fishing villages, quiet beaches and fewer than 1,000 permanent residents, the islands have a relaxed, laid-back charm. The best sandy beach is at Šunj on Lopud.

➕ 198 B1

🔟 Lokrum

Just 15 minutes by boat from Dubrovnik, the wooded isle of Lokrum (see walk on pages 180–182) makes a popular half-day outing. The English king Richard the Lionheart (1157–99) is said to have been shipwrecked here on his way back from the Crusades, while in the 19th century the island was a summer retreat for Archduke Maximilian von Habsburg, younger brother of the Austro-Hungarian emperor Franz Josef I, who converted the old Benedictine monastery into a private villa and laid out the formal gardens, still visited today.

There is good swimming here, both in the warm saltwater lake known as the Mrtvo More (Dead Sea) and from the spectacularly sited

naturist beach on the east side of the island, signposted from the jetty. Boats depart regularly for Lokrum in summer from the old harbour at Dubrovnik; in winter, there are occasional weekend excursions, or you may find a taxi-boat to take you.

➕ 198 B1

9️⃣ Cavtat

Cavtat is less than 20km (12 miles) south of Dubrovnik and only a few minutes from the airport. It is one of Croatia's prettiest resorts, set around a horseshoe bay enclosed by peninsulas on both sides, with views to the isle of Supetar and Dubrovnik in the distance. In the 3rd century BC, this was the Greek town of Epidaurum; a thousand years later, its inhabitants fled northwards to found Dubrovnik.

The painter Vlaho Bukovac (1855–1922) was born here and you can visit his house and studio on the waterfront; his image of 19th-century Cavtat harbour can be seen above the chancel in the nearby Church of Our Lady of the Snows. A path from here leads to the summit of the Rat peninsula, the original site of Greek Epidaurum, where you will find the domed Račić mausoleum, designed by Ivan Meštrović for a local shipping magnate.

With cafés on the palm-lined promenade and 5km (3 miles) of seafront paths linking beaches and pine woods, Cavtat makes a good base for a relaxing seaside holiday. Boats depart regularly throughout the summer for the old harbour in Dubrovnik.

➕ 198 C1
🚌 Bus 10 from Dubrovnik
Tourist Information Office
✉ Tiha 3 ☎ 020 479025

Where to... Stay

Prices

Expect to pay per person per night for a double room

€ under 250kn   €€ 250kn–500kn   €€€ over 500kn

CAVTAT

Supetar €€

This small, attractive hotel is set in an old stone house on the waterfront, with lovely views across the bay to the Sustjepan Peninsula. It is just a short distance from a pebble beach and concrete bathing platform, though guests also have access to the swimming pool at the Hotel Croatia, a large, luxury five-star hotel belonging to the same company on the other side of the bay. The cafés and restaurants are a few minutes away, as is the harbour, where boats depart regularly for Dubrovnik.

➕ 198 C1 ⊠ Obala Stjepana Radića
☎ 020 479833; www.hoteli-croatia.hr/supetar

DUBROVNIK

There are just two small hotels inside the old city of Dubrovnik. Most of the top hotels are outside the Ploče Gate, while the majority of package accommodation is on the Lapad and Babin Kuk peninsulas, 5km (3 miles) west of the city, or in the resorts of Cavtat, Mlini and Plat to the south.

Grand Villa Argentina €€€

The guest list at the Argentina has included Tito, Margaret Thatcher, Richard Burton and Elizabeth Taylor. The hotel, traditionally considered the top address in town, is made up of four separate villas, including the lovely 1930s Villa Orsula and the early 20th-century folly Villa Scheherazade, as well as a modern building. Steps lead down through the gardens to a small private beach; there are also outdoor seawater and heated indoor pools. The sea-facing rooms have views to the old town, a 10-minute walk away.

➕ 202 off C2 ⊠ Frana Supila 14
☎ 020 440555;
www.hoteli-argentina.hr

Hilton Imperial €€€

One of Dubrovnik's earliest hotels, built in 1895 just outside the Pile Gate, reopened in 2005 under the management of the Hilton chain. The Imperial combines art nouveau architecture and charm with all the modern facilities you would expect, including an indoor pool and fitness club with saunas and Jacuzzis. The rooms have wood and marble fittings; some have balconies with sea views.

➕ 202 off A2 ⊠ Ulica Dr Ante Starčevića ☎ 020 320320;
www.hilton.com

Hotel Sumartin €€

This old-style hotel on the Lapad Peninsula was built in 1922 and has been restored and upgraded. The comfortable rooms, set in a handsome three-floor villa surrounded by tall palm trees, are furnished simply. The pebble beach at Lapad cove is a short walk away, and there are regular buses to Pile Gate.

➕ 202 off A2 ⊠ Šetalište Kralja Zvonimira 31 ☎ 020 436146
🚌 Bus 5, 6, 7

Pucić Palace €€€

This five-star boutique hotel opened in 2003 in an 18th-century palace overlooking the market square in the old town. It's a gem of a place, whose atmosphere of informal luxury set the trend for small town-house hotels in Croatia. The 19 rooms have original artworks, antique furniture, handwoven rugs and dark oak parquet floors, along with modern conveniences such as DVD players and satellite TV. Dining options include a boulevard café, wine bar and terrace restaurant serving Middle Eastern cuisine. The hotel has its own private yacht which is available for guests to rent.

✚ 202 B1 ☒ Ulica Od Puča 1
☎ 020 326200;
www.thepucipalace.com

Stari Grad €€€

The only other place to stay within the old town walls is this small hotel, with just eight rooms, in an old aristocratic mansion close to the Pile Gate. Its old mirrors, chandeliers, antique furnishings and rugs lend it a great deal of charm. A highlight is the small roof terrace, with magnificent views over the city.

✚ 202 A2 ☒ Od Sigurate 4 ☎ 020 322244; www.hotelstarigrad.com

Vila Curić €€

If you don't mind being outside the city, these 14 modern self-catering apartments are in a quiet street on the Babin Kuk peninsula, on a hill overlooking Gruž harbour and the bridge at Rijeka Dubrovačka. Each of the apartments has a kitchen, bathroom and living-room, and some have a balcony or terrace. There is also a handful of double rooms. The beaches and promenades of Babin Kuk are close by and the old city is a bus ride away, making this a good place to combine a seaside holiday with a city break.

✚ 202 off A2 ☒ Ulica Mostarska 2
☎ 020 436555; www.vila-curic.hr
🚌 Bus 6

Villa Dubrovnik €€€

This intimate and romantic hotel is set in a low-rise white Modernist villa, among gardens of orange and lemon trees on the cliffs about 1km (0.6 mile) east of the old city. Each of the 40 rooms has a balcony with a sea view, and the restaurant terrace overlooks the sea and the isle of Lokrum. Steps lead down to a private beach, and guests can take a free shuttle boat from the hotel to the old harbour in summer; otherwise it's a 30-minute walk. Note that between mid-July and mid-September half-board (lunch or dinner) is compulsory, at extra cost.

✚ 202 off C2 ☒ Ulica Vlaha Bukovca 6 ☎ 020 422933; www.villa-dubrovnik.hr
🕓 Mar–Nov

KORČULA

Korčula €€

The large package hotels are on the fringes of Korčula town, but if you want to be more central, the best choice is the Korčula. With 20 rooms in a white stone building, 1912, it stands just outside the town walls, beside one of the entrances to the old town. Be sure to have an evening drink on the west-facing waterfront terrace, which is perfectly placed to catch the sunset.

✚ 199 F2 ☒ Obala Vinka Paletina, Korčula town
☎ 020 711078; www.htp-korcula.hr

MLJET

Odisej €€

The only large hotel on the island is inside Mljet National Park, beside a small cove in the pretty seaside village of Pomena. The 156 rooms are spread out across a number of whitewashed pavilions, and there are also two apartments with their own kitchenette, living-room and balcony with sea view. This is a good base for an active holiday, with scuba diving and sailing courses and bicycles for rent. A short walk from Pomena leads through the woods to Malo Jezero, the smaller of the park's two saltwater lakes.

✚ 198 A1 ☒ Pomena ☎ 020 744022; www.hotelodisej.hr

Where to...
Eat and Drink

Prices

Expect to pay for a three-course meal for one, excluding drinks and service

€ under 100kn   €€ 100kn–150kn   €€€ over 150kn

CAVTAT

Galija €€€

This old-style tavern and wine cellar is on a cobbled street leading uphill towards the cemetery. You can eat indoors in winter, but the main attraction on summer evenings is the beautiful seaside terrace, with tables set with candles and fine linen beneath the pine trees. The Dalmatian food and wine are first-class, from the free starter of fish pâté to smoked ham, seafood risotto, boiled sea-bass, grilled fish and barbecued steaks. More

inventive offerings might include sea-urchins, shrimps in honey or carpaccio of grouper with parmesan and rocket (arugula), an excellent choice for a celebration meal.

✚ 198 C1 ☒ Vuličeviceva 1 ☎ 020 478566 ⊘ Daily 11am–1am, Mar–Oct

DUBROVNIK

Buffet Škola €

The tiny Buffet Škola, just off the Stradun, makes the best sandwiches in town. Nothing fancy: just thick slices of crusty home-made bread filled with Dalmatian ham or cheese in oil and tomato. You can find it at

the foot of a narrow alley leading up towards Prijeko. In summer there are a couple of tables out on the street for alfresco snacking.

✚ 202 B2 ☒ Antuninska 1 ☎ 020 321096 ⊘ Daily 8am–3am

Lokanda Peskarija €

Locals come here for good, fresh, simply cooked seafood, right beside the harbour and the old fish market. Choose from mussels, prawns, oysters, squid, grilled fish or seafood risotto, served with salad and dry white wine. Get here early at lunchtime, or be prepared to wait.

✚ 202 C1 ☒ Na Ponti ☎ 020 324750 ⊘ Daily 8am–midnight

Mea Culpa €

For a good value lunch, you can't beat this popular pizzeria in the back streets of the old town. The pizzas are cooked in a wood-fired oven; other choices include lasagne and salads. There are a few tables inside, but most people eat outside on the cobbled street.

✚ 202 A1 ☒ Za Rokom 3 ☎ 020 424819 ⊘ Daily 8am–midnight

Orhan €€€

This smart fish restaurant outside the Pile Gate is one of Dubrovnik's best-kept secrets. Take the steps down to the waterfront beneath the Lovrijenac Fortress and you will find it among the upturned fishing boats, beside a peaceful cove which once served as the city's main harbour. On summer evenings, you can dine on a covered terrace right beside the sea. The house special is fresh fish, brought to your table on a tray to help you make your choice. If you don't want the fish, other options include steaks, schnitzels, risottos and pasta dishes.

✚ 202 off A2 ☒ Od Tabakarije 1 ☎ 020 414183 ⊘ Daily 11am–midnight

Rozarij €€

Tucked away in a corner at the end of Prijeko, Rozarij is far more intimate and discreet than the rows of identical tourist restaurants along the rest of Prijeko. In summer, tables are put outside on the terrace in front of the Church of St Nicholas and along the narrow passageway leading to the Dominican monastery. The restaurant serves Dalmatian staples, such as grilled fish, steak and cuttlefish risotto, along with generous salads and excellent Turkish coffee to finish.

➕ 202 B2 ⊠ Prijeko 2 ☎ 020 321257 ⏰ Daily 11am–midnight

Sesame €€

This buzzy, arty bistro outside the Pile Gate is popular with students. The walls are lined with old theatre posters and programmes for the Dubrovnik Summer Festival dating back 50 years, as well as a grenade from the 1991–2 war. The Mediterranean menu is strong on pasta dishes, and unusual salads such as smoked ham with figs or octopus with cheese. Vegetarians are well catered for – try the

vegetable sorbet or courgette carpaccio followed by pasta with truffles.

➕ 202 off A2 ⊠ Ulica Dante Aligherija ☎ 020 412190 ⏰ Daily 8am–11pm

KORČULA

Adio Mare €€

The most atmospheric place to eat in Korčula is this down-to-earth tavern near the cathedral, with stone walls and communal wooden tables and benches. The menu, which has hardly changed for 30 years, features Dalmatian classics like *brudet* (fish soup with polenta), *pržolica* (stewed veal with onions, tomatoes and prunes), along with steaks and kebabs which are barbecued on live coal on an open fire in the corner. There are no reservations, so arrive early.

➕ 199 F2 ⊠ Ulica Svetog Roka 2, Korčula town ☎ 020 711253 ⏰ Daily 6pm–midnight, May–Oct

Maslina €

Set among olive groves on the road from Korčula to Lumbarda, this small family-run restaurant serves up excellent home-cooked food and is one of the few places on the island to stay open throughout the year. House specials include macaroni and *pogača*, a pizza-like dish of crusty bread topped with tomatoes, onions, peppers, aubergines, courgettes, olive tapenade and melted cheese. You can eat outside on the terrace in summer but there is no sea view – the restaurant is right beside the road.

➕ 199 F2 ⊠ Lumbarajska Cesta ☎ 020 711720 ⏰ Daily 11am–midnight in summer; 5pm–midnight in winter

Morski Konjic €€

This long terrace restaurant takes up virtually the whole of the eastern promenade, with tables on the sea walls looking across the water to the Pelješac peninsula. The wide-ranging menu includes meat and

fish dishes such as plain grilled fish, mussels and octopus salad, washed down with the local Grk and Pošip wines.

➕ 199 F2 ⊠ Šetalište Petra Kanavelića ☎ 020 711878 ⏰ Daily 8am–1am, Apr–Oct

PELJEŠAC

Kapetanova Kuća €€€

People come from far and wide to sample the local oysters at Mali Ston, which are famed for their aphrodisiac qualities. There are several good restaurants on the picturesque waterfront but the captain's house' is the best, offering fresh and grilled oysters, oyster soup and beef in oyster sauce, as well as local mussels, lobster and fresh fish. Mali Ston has become a popular honeymoon destination and the same owners run a small boutique hotel, Hotel Ostrea.

➕ 198 B1 ⊠ Mali Ston ☎ 020 754264 ⏰ Daily 9am–midnight

Where to... Shop

DUBROVNIK

The shops along Stradun are designed to appeal mainly to tourists to Dubrovnik, offering T-shirts, souvenirs, postcards, books and CDs. For a wide range of foreign-language books about Croatia, check out the branch of **Algoritam** (Stradun 8). If you are interested, most of the bookshops in the old town sell English-language books and videos about Dubrovnik at war during the siege of 1991–2.

To seek out the more unusual boutiques, you need to leave Stradun and explore the narrow streets to the south, especially on and around **Od Puča**. This is the main shopping street of the old town, with small offbeat shops

specializing in costume jewellery, men's and women's fashions, antiques and modern art. Several shops at the western end of **Od Puča** sell intricate gold and silver jewellery in filigree designs, a speciality of Dubrovnik since the days of the Ragusan republic. If you're after a silk tie, a branch of **Croata** is at Pred Dvorom 2, beside the cathedral. The pharmacy in the cloisters of the **Franjevački Samostan** (Franciscan monastery ►147) sells herbal remedies and potions which are said to date back to 1317.

The morning market in **Poljana Gundulićeva**, at the eastern end of Od Puča, is a lively affair, with farmers selling cheeses, fruit liqueurs and pretty little strings of dried figs, as well as fresh produce.

For Dalmatian wines and spirits, check out **Vinoteka** (Stradun) or **Dubrovačka Kuća** (Ulica Svetog Dominika), a wine shop and art gallery not far inside the Ploče Gate.

Where to... Be Entertained

CAVTAT

Look out for performances of *klapa*, male-voice choirs who perform without instruments; concerts are held outside the parish church on summer evenings.

DUBROVNIK

During the **Dubrovnik Summer Festival** more than 80 performances of drama, opera, music and ballet taking place at open-air stages in the old city. The festival starts each year with a fireworks display on 10 July and finishes on 25 August. For information and tickets, contact the festival office (tel: 020 326100; www.dubrovnik-festival.hr) or visit the kiosks at

Stradun and Pile Gate.

The monthly *Dubrovnik Guide* gives details of other events. During the summer months, the Lindo folk ensemble perform traditional songs and dances on Tuesday and Friday evenings at Lazareti, the former quarantine hospital outside the Ploče Gate. Jazz fans should head for Troubadour, a bar in Buničeva Poljana. There is live jazz at 10pm most nights in summer.

KORČULA

The *moreška* sword dance (►26–27) is performed Monday and Thursday evenings in summer beside the Land Gate and at festivals, with the biggest on 29 July. Tickets from local travel agents.

Walks & Tours

1 Zagreb Old Town

Walk

DISTANCE 2.7km (1.6 miles) TIME 1–1.5 hours
START/END POINT Trg Bana Jelačića ➕ 201 D3

This short walk, beginning and ending in Zagreb's central square, explores the oldest and most attractive part of the capital – the maze of narrow streets and squares known as Gornji Grad (Upper Town). A funicular tramway takes you up the hill, avoiding a steep ascent on foot. Although it is possible to complete this walk in an hour, it is best to allow half a day to enjoy the various churches and museums along the way, go shopping in Dolac market and soak up the atmosphere of this historic district.

1–2

Start in **Trg Bana Jelačića** (➤ 46–48) beside the statue of Governor Josip Jelačić on horseback. With your back to the statue, face half-right and head for Dubrovnik Kavana, with outdoor tables on the corner of Ulica Ljudevita Gaja (also known as Gajeva, ➤ 166 panel). This is the entrance to a busy

pedestrianized area of shops, cafés and ice-cream parlours which is particularly animated on summer evenings. Walk down Gajeva and turn right opposite the glass façade of the

The funicular connecting the Upper and Lower towns

Hotel Dubrovnik into Ulica Mirka Bogovića (Bogovićeva), Zagreb's principal promenading street, lined with open-air cafés and bars. The street ends in Trg Petra Preradovića, a large square with more cafés and a cinema.

2–3

Turn right here, passing the statue of Petar Preradović (1818–72), a soldier and romantic poet. Just beyond the statue is the Serbian Orthodox Church, the meeting place of the city's Serbian minority, which remained remarkably untouched during the conflict with Serbia in the 1990s. Emerging on Ilica, Zagreb's main shopping street, turn left and take the first right into Ulica Tomića (Tomićeva).

3–4

take the funicular (*uspinjača*), which runs every 10 minutes from 6:30am to 9pm. This delightful ride, the oldest form of public transport in Zagreb, first opened in 1893 as a steam-powered railway and was electrified in 1934. With a speed of 1.5m per second and a journey time of under a minute, it is sometimes said to be the shortest public transport journey in the world. Alternatively, you can climb the flight of steps beside the tramway to reach the upper town of Gradec.

4–5

Emerging from the funicular station, a leafy promenade, Strossmayerovo Šetalište, runs both left and right, following the route of the old city walls. Instead, keep straight

ahead, passing to the right of the Tower of Lotršćak with a glimpse of the coloured roof tiles of St Mark's Church (Sv. Marka) up ahead. Take the first left along Ulica Vranicanijeva and turn right along Ulica Matoša (Matoševa), passing the Hrvatski Povijesni Muzej (Croatian History Museum) on your left.

5–6

At the end of this street, turn left and immediately right onto Ulica Mesnička, where you will see the Prirodoslovni Muzej (Natural History Museum), an eclectic collection housed in an old theatre, on your left. Follow this street until you reach

Map labels: BRANJUGOVA, KAPTOL, GRAD, Kaptol, Tkalčićeva, Stjepana Radića, Opatička, Demetrova, Fondacija Ivan Meštrović, Prirodoslovni Muzej, Mesnička, Strossm. Šetalište, Naivne Umjetnosti, Hrvatski Muzej, Sv. Marka, Matoševa, Markov trg, kam., Sabor, Kamenita Vrata, Habdelić, Katarinin Trg, Sv. Katerina, Uspinjača, Kula Lotršćak, Tomićeva, ILICA, Trg Petra Preradovića, Bogovićeva, Gajeva, Dolac, Pod zidom, Trg Bana Jelačića, Trg A. Stepinca, Bakačeva, PRAŠKA, Katedrala, JURIŠIĆEVA, AMRUŠEVA, N TESLE, MASARYKOVA

6, 5, 8, 7, 9, 4, 3, 2, 1, 10, i

0 200 metres
0 200 yards

a Classical-style archway leading to a school. Turn right here along Ulica Mletačka, passing the Fondacija Ivan Meštrović (▶ 52–53) on your left. Turn left at the end of the street to enter Markov trg (St Mark's Square).

6–7

This square is the symbolic heart of Croatia, lined with baroque palaces and government buildings. On one side is the Sabor (Croatian parliament), on the other the offices of the presidency in the former Banski Dvor (Governor's Palace). It was this building that was hit by a Serbian rocket attack in October 1991, when President Tudman was meeting here with his cabinet – an event described in detail in the **City Museum** (▶ 54).

Cross to the far side of the square for the best views of St Mark's Church, then continue walking downhill in the direction of the Tower of Lotrščak, passing the **Hrvatski Muzej Naivne Umjetnosti** (Naïve Art Museum, ▶ 54) and Greek Orthodox Church of St Cyril and St Methodius on your right. Returning to the crossroads just before the tower, turn left to see St Catherine's Church (Sv. Katerina) ahead of you. This is the city's baroque masterpiece, its façade featuring sculptures of the Virgin and the four evangelists.

Street Names

Most streets in Zagreb have at least two different names – the one seen on street signs and the one used in conversation and on maps. Thus Ulica Gaja becomes Gajeva, Ulica Bogovića becomes Bogovićeva, Ulica Tomića becomes Tomićeva, Ulica Radica becomes Radićeva and Ulica Tkalčića becomes Tkalčićeva. To confuse matters further, the square which is officially known as Trg Petra Preradovića, near the start of this walk, is universally referred to by the locals as Cvijetni Trg (Flower Square) because of the flower market that used to be held there.

7–8

Turn left beside the church to enter Jezuitski Trg, where the former Jesuit monastery is now an art gallery hosting temporary exhibitions. At the crossroads, notice the old pharmacy on the corner of Ulica Kamenita, in business since the mid-14th century. Turn right to walk through the Kamenita Vrata (Stone Gate), one of the four original entrances to the walled

As you walk through Zagreb, look out for details such as this wall sign on Ulica Kaptol

The richly decorated nave of St Catherine's Church, in the Upper Town

town of Gradec. According to legend, after much of the old town was destroyed by fire in 1731, a painting of the Virgin Mary was discovered undamaged in the ashes. To celebrate this miracle, the gate was rebuilt and it now houses a shrine, full of flickering candles and devout pilgrims at prayer.

8–9

After passing through the gate, take the steps to the right beside the George and Dragon statue and turn right along Ulica Radića (Radićeva), a steep cobbled street lined with art galleries and souvenir shops. Turn left onto Krvavi Most (Bloody Bridge), the historic boundary between the townships of Kaptol and Gradec, whose name reflects the violent confrontations that used to take place between the two. Looking up, the spires of the cathedral are visible above the houses. Cross the bridge to reach Ulica Tkalčića (Tkalčićeva), one of the city's most attractive streets, but being repaved, whose 19th-century houses are now home to fashionable boutiques and trendy, youthful bars. The

street lies on the dried-up channel of the former stream which once separated Kaptol from Gradec.

9–10

Turn left and then right onto Ulica Skalinska to arrive on the upper level of Dolac market, with clothes stalls in the street to your left and farmers selling fresh produce down below. Take the steps down to the main market square and continue in the same direction towards the **katedrala** (cathedral, ► 50). When you reach the street named Kaptol, with the cathedral directly ahead of you, turn right to return to Trg Bana Jelačića.

Taking a Break

Mala Kavana, on the north side of Trg Bana Jelačića close to the equestrian statue, is an old-style café serving good coffee and cakes. For drinks, just take your pick of the trendy bars along Ulica Tkalčića (Tkalčićeva). A good place for lunch is **Kerempuh** (► 61), on the upper level of Dolac market.

2 Zagorje
Tour

This scenic drive makes a circuit of the Zagorje (► 73–75), a bucolic region of cornfields, meadows, vineyards, pretty villages, hilltop churches and fairy-tale castles between Zagreb and the Slovenian border. Although you could easily spend several days exploring this region, it is possible to cover the main sights in a day-trip from

DISTANCE 148km (92 miles), plus 10km (6 miles) with the divrsion to Trakošćan
TIME 3.5 hours
START/END POINT Marija Bistrica ✛ 194 C4

Zagreb, adding around two hours to the total time.

1–2
Start in the pilgrimage town of **Marija Bistrica** (► 74) and take the road to Donja Stubica. The road out of town is not well signposted, so it is easier to take the main road to Zagreb south from the church and turn right when you reach a junction on the edge of town. Stay on this gentle road as it winds through the peaceful Stubica valley beneath the northern slopes of **mount Medvednica** (► 59), whose TV mast is visible on the summit. The first village of any size is Gornja Stubica, known as the birthplace of a Peasant's Revolt in 1573, which is commemorated in the Muzej Seljačkih Buna (Museum of Peasant Uprisings). Shortly afterwards, you reach the lovely village

of Donja Stubica, where a road beside the church square leads to the summit of Sljeme, making a spectacular drive to Zagreb.

2–3

Continue on this road through the spa town of Stubičke Toplice, where the road bends right, following signs to Zabok. After a further 2km (1.2 miles), turn left at a roundabout towards Zabok. The road crosses the Zagreb-Krapina motorway, bypasses Zabok and continues for 20km (12.5 miles) to **Kumrovec** (▶ 82), rising and then falling to the dramatic Sutla valley, right on the Slovenian border. Shortly before Kumrovec, you enter the Zelenjak Gorge, with the forested hills of Slovenia visible across the river. On your right, you pass the Lijepa Naša monument, a stone obelisk dedicated to local poet Antun Mihanović (1796–1861), the author of the Croatian national anthem (▶ 170).

3–4

Just after passing Kumrovec, you reach a fork in the road, where you must keep right to Miljana – a left fork would take you to a Slovenian border post instead. Note the hill-top church on the horizon, high above the

perched on a hill to your left. After exploring the castle, drive through the village of Desinić and take the left fork towards Pregrada.

5–6

Arriving in Pregrada, turn right along the main street, following signs to Zagreb. After 5km (3 miles), turn left beside the Dvorec Bežanec hotel (▶ 86) and stay on this road as it rises and falls through the vineyards, before dropping steeply to Krapina.

Lace-making is a regional speciality

thickly wooded slopes. Now you are in the rural heart of the Zagorje, all farm-steads, barns and roadside shrines, and cottages offering *seoski turizam* (agrotourism; ▶ 16–18). The road climbs to the village of Zagorska Sela, domi-nated by the Church of Sveta Katerina, and continues to Miljana.

4–5

Turn right here towards Desinić or you will soon reach another border post. Shortly you will see the castle of **Veliki Tabor** (▶ 73)

oversized, cream-coloured church.
A short diversion left at this point leads in 5km (3 miles) to the castle at Trakošćan (➤ 74).

7–8
To complete the main route return to Bednja and turn right towards Lepoglava, the site of a notorious prison where both Tito and Franjo Tudman were incarcerated. The prison, the largest in Croatia, occupies the site of a former monastery, built by the Pauline order of monks who also established Croatia's first grammar school and university here. In Lepoglava, turn right and follow the railway line for the next 5km (3 miles). Reaching a junction, turn left, passing through Zlatar and Zlatar Bistrica on the way back to Marija Bistrica.

Taking a Break
Grešna Gorica (Taborgradska 3, Desinić, tel: 049 343001, daily 10–10, ➤ 87).

The walkway beneath the castle walls at Trakošćan

The Croatian National Anthem
Croatia's national anthem is *Lijepa Naša Domovino* (Our Beautiful Homeland). The words were written by Antun Mihanović in 1835. It was first performed as the national anthem in 1891 and was readopted in 1990, shortly before independence from Yugoslavia.

Our beautiful homeland,
O so fearless, our beloved country,
Our fathers' ancient glory,
Shall always be blessed!

You are our only glory,
You are our only treasure,
We love your plains and valleys,
We love your hills and mountains.

6–7
Turn left as you enter Krapina, passing the Museum of Evolution on your left. Continue on this road as it runs beside the railway line, then turn right, signposted to Varaždin, passing beneath the busy motorway high overhead. Stay on this minor country road to reach the village of Bednja, with its

3 Istrian Hill Towns

Tour

DISTANCE 68km (42 miles) **TIME** 1.5 hours
START/END POINT Pazin ✚ 192 B4

Although they lie just a short distance inland from the busy coastal resorts, the hill towns of Istria offer a completely different experience. Even if you are staying by the sea in Poreč, Pula or Rovinj, it is worth renting a car for the day and heading inland among the vineyards, olive groves and oak woods. This short, easy circuit takes in two of the most dramatic hill towns, though it can easily be extended to include others (▶ 103) or taken as a leisurely half-day excursion from the coast.

1–2

Begin in **Pazin**, which can be reached on the fast highway connecting Rijeka with Rovinj and Pula. This small industrious town of

The fortified walls of the hilltop town of Buzet

around 10,000 inhabitants may not have immediate appeal, but it repays an hour or two of exploration. The highlight is the castle, first mentioned in AD 983 as a gift of Emperor Otto II of Hungary to the bishop of Poreč. The castle, which now contains an ethnographic museum (Tue–Sun 10–6, in summer, reduced hours in winter), overlooks a great gorge known as Pazin's Pit, where the River Pazinčica swells after rain, almost encircling the town.

Although he never visited Pazin, the French novelist Jules Verne (1828–1905) was inspired by the pit – the hero of his novel, Mathias Sandorf, was imprisoned in the castle and escaped by swimming along the underground river and into the sea.

Leave Pazin by taking the main road through the middle of town in the direction of Rijeka and the Učka Tunnel. After 2km (1.2 miles), you will see a right turn leading to the motorway to Rijeka. Ignore this and keep straight ahead, crossing fertile countryside with the peaks of Učka, often covered in snow, rising in the distance. After 8km (5 miles), you come to the village of Cerovlje, best known for its brickworks.

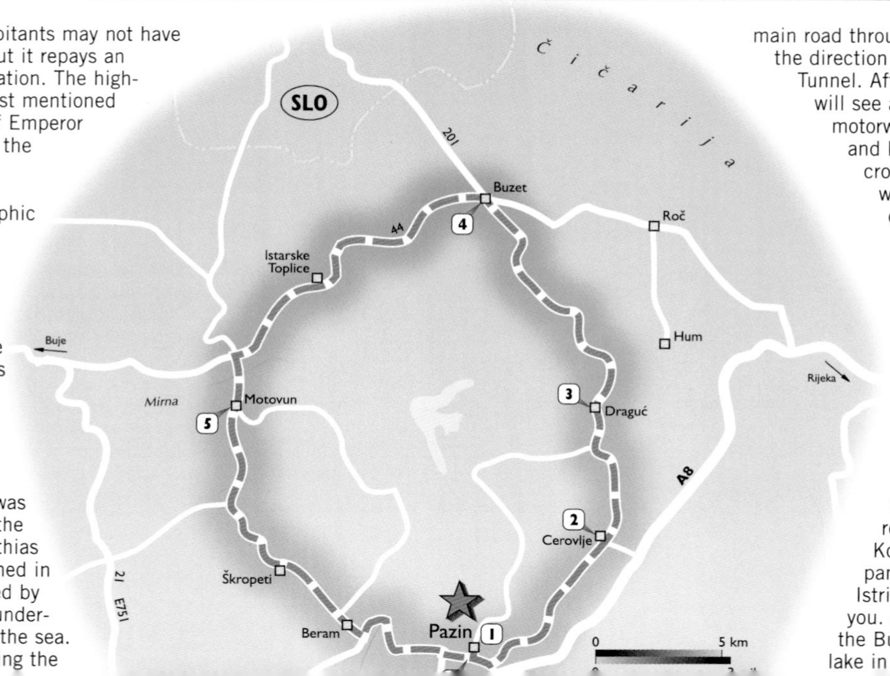

2–3

Turn left immediately before the level crossing on the old road to Buzet, and left again at the next junction. The road now rises to Kovačići, where a panoramic view of central Istria opens out in front of you. Ahead and to the left is the Butoniga valley, with a lake in the middle and views

Č i č a r i j a

Rijeka →

Roč

Hum

Draguć

A8

Buzet

201

④

③

②

Cerovlje

SLO

Istarske
Toplice

AA

★ Pazin ①

Beram

Motovun

Škropeti

Mirma

⑤

Buje →

21 E751

0 _____ 5 km

across the plain to the hill town of Motovun in the distance; to the right is the great Ćićarija ridge, dividing Istria from Slovenia and the rest of Croatia.

Shortly afterwards, you reach the village of Draguć, little more than a single street of houses and a tall church perched on a cliff. In the 1970s and 1980s, Draguć was known as the 'Istrian Hollywood' as a number of films were shot here, but these days the village is largely deserted. The 12th-century Romanesque Chapel of St Elisium and the 14th-century Church of St Rock are both renowned for their frescoes; the latter, painted by Master Anthony of Padova, features vivid images of biblical scenes including the Adoration of the Magi and the Annunciation. The churches are normally kept locked, but if you ask around in the village you may find the keyholder who will let you in for a small donation.

Glagolitic Alley

A short diversion along the road from Buzet to Rijeka leads to Roč, the start of the so-called 'Glagolitic Alley'. This 7km (4-mile) sculpture trail between Roč and Hum commemorates the Glagolitic script, a 41-letter Slavonic alphabet devised in the 9th century by the Greek brothers St Cyril and St Methodius, who were instrumental in converting Croatia to Christianity. The script was widely used in liturgical texts in Croatia between the 11th and 19th centuries, and the first known printing of a Glagolitic missal took place in Istria in 1483. Eleven sculptures along the trail recall important events and symbols in Istrian and Croatian history. Look out for the stone featuring the Glagolitic, Latin and Cyrillic alphabets – Glagolitic was a forerunner of Cyrillic, which is named after St Cyril and is still used in Russia, Bulgaria and Serbia. The trail ends in Hum, the self-proclaimed and somewhat self-conscious 'smallest town in the world', with just 20 inhabitants, an annual election for mayor and a copper town gate engraved in the Glagolitic script.

One of the stones along the Glagolitic Alley depicting a letter of the Slavonic alphabet

3–4

The road continues as far as Buzet, the largest of the hill towns, on a bluff 151m (495 feet) above the River Mirna and still partly enclosed by its medieval walls and gates. In recent years, Buzet has become Istria's self-styled 'city of truffles' and each autumn it attracts visitors who come here to taste and buy this expensive delicacy.

4–5

At Buzet, turn left to follow the main road along the Mirna valley towards Buje. You pass the spa town of Istarske Toplice, whose waters have been known for their healing properties since Roman times. Stay on this road as it continues through the narrow valley with oak woods and tall crags to either side. When you reach a crossroads, turn left and take the bridge across the river towards Motovun (▶ 103), the best known and most spectacularly sited of the Istrian hill towns. After another 2km (1.2 miles), you can park at the foot of the hill and climb to Motovun, or pay a toll in summer to drive up.

Crozjnan – one of the area's hill towns

5–6

Stay on this road and turn left at a junction to return to Pazin. Along the way you pass the small village of Beram, noted for its 15th-century cycle of frescoes. They are in the chapel of the Virgin Mary just outside the village, and feature a macabre Dance of the Dead, depicting not only skeletons, but a rich gallery of human characters from medieval Istria. The message, of course, is that all humans are equal at the hour of death.

Taking a Break

Hotel Kaštel (▶ 108)
✚ 192 B4
✉ Trg Andrea Antico 7, Motovun
☎ 052 681607
🕐 Daily 8am–10pm
💷 Moderate

Barbacan (▶ 110)
✚ 192 B4
✉ Ulica Barbacan 1, Motovun
☎ 052 681791
🕐 Tue–Sun 11–11, Mar–Nov
💷 Moderate

4 Dubrovnik Old Town

Walk

DISTANCE 3km (1 mile) **TIME** 1 hour
START/END POINT Vrata od Pile (Pile Gate)
🔒 202 A2

The classic walk in Dubrovnik may be the circuit of the city walls (▶ 148), but it can be just as rewarding to stroll inside the ramparts, discovering hidden lanes and courtyards in the oldest parts of the city. Even when Stradun is thronging with visitors, it is usually possible to find a quiet corner just a few streets away. This short walk explores the narrow lanes rising above Stradun to either side, so involves a fair degree of climbing. Most local buses stop outside Pile Gate, the start point for the walk; arriving by boat from Cavtat at the old harbour, you need to walk the length of Stradun to reach the start.

1–2

Begin just inside Pile Gate beside the Onofrio Fountain. This large domed structure, with water spouting from sculpted masks, is a popular meeting place where buskers

Medieval Graffiti

From Ulica Od Puča, near the start of the walk, a few steps right along Ulica Zlatarica lead to one of Dubrovnik's hidden gems. Look carefully and you will see some graffiti, dated 1597, etched into the outside wall of the Church of St Rock. Translated from the Latin, it serves as a warning to children playing ball in the street: 'I'm warning you, players..peace be with you, but remember that you will die'.

entertain the crowds. The fountain was completed in 1444 by the Neapolitan engineer Onofrio della Cava to supply fresh water to the city. It was badly damaged during the earthquake of 1667 and again during the siege of 1991–2, but has now been restored to its former glory. The nearby

The Pile Gate entrance into the walled city

Church of Sveti Spasa (St Saviour) is used for summer evening concerts.

Walk straight ahead along Stradun, whose limestone paving has been polished to a sheen by the many footsteps passing this way over the centuries. Almost immediately, look for an archway to your right and pass beneath the arch into Ulica Gariste. At the next cross-roads, turn left into Ulica Od Puča, the main shopping street of the old town. There are several good jewellery shops here selling the distinctive local gold and silver filigree work, as well as art galleries, haberdashers and wine shops.

2–3
Turn right at Ulica Široka, passing Dom Marina Držića, the former home of the play-wright Marin Držić (1508–67) on your left. Držić was known for his bawdy comedies, performed in the fashionable Renaissance salons of Dubrovnik, Venice and Zagreb. The house is now a museum, with audiovisual displays giving an insight into 16th-century society. Continue straight ahead and climb the steps beside the Domino steak house, then turn right along Ulica Od Rupa. A short distance along on your left is the Etnografski Muzej Rupe, an ethnographic museum in the

Strolling the city walls

former city granary, with deep storage pits carved out of the rock. The terrace in front of the museum has fine views over the city, sheltering beneath the bulk of Mount Srd.

3–4
Turn left alongside the museum to ascend the narrow staircase of Ulica Od Sorte. As you climb, notice the protruding stone struts on the fronts of the houses, with pierced holes through which washing lines would be suspended for drying laundry or woollen yarn (Dubrovnik was known for its textiles in medieval times). At the top of the street, turn left to walk beside the former Benedictine convent of St Mary. After being ransacked and dissolved by Napoleonic troops during the French occupation (1805–15), the convent became a barracks and later a mili-tary hospital, and is now an apartment block. The entrance to the main courtyard features a relief of the Annunciation beneath the coats of arms of Dubrovnik and noble families.

Stay on this cobbled path through one of the oldest and highest districts of the city until you come to some peaceful garden allot-ments beneath the city walls. The path now drops steeply beside the walls and a gap in the wall to your right (incongruously signposted 'Cold Drinks' in English) leads to a bar in a stunning location. It is certainly worth spending an hour here in summer, sitting beneath a palm tree on the side of the cliffs and gazing at the isle of Lokrum across the sea.

4–5

Keep beside the walls as they bend left beneath the bastion of Sveta Margarita.

Looking to your left, you can see the Jesuit Church (Isusovačka) dominating the market square of Poljana Rudera Boškovića. Completed in 1725, this is the largest church in Dubrovnik, its interior a riot of baroque excess with marble altars and mosaic tiles. Cross the square and walk down the

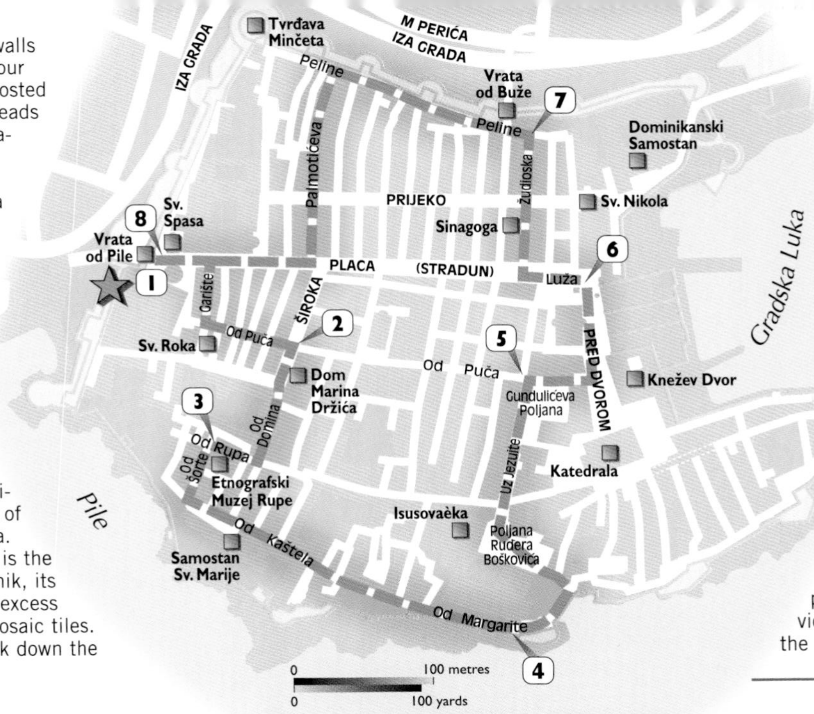

monumental Jesuit Steps, built in 1738 to provide a suitably grand approach to the church and based on the Spanish Steps in Rome.

The steps end in Gundulićeva Poljana, which is busy each morning with farmers selling fresh fruit, vegetables and herbs, as well as bottles of lavender oil and strings of dried peppers and figs. At the heart of the square is a statue of Ivan Gundulić (1589–1638), Dubrovnik's greatest poet and a key figure in Croatian literature. The pedestal is decorated with scenes from his best-known poem, *Osman*, describing a victory for the Polish army over the Ottoman Turks.

Map labels: Gradska Luka · Dominikanski Samostan · Sv. Nikola · Knežev Dvor · PRED DVOROM · Katedrala · Gundulićeva Poljana · Uz Jezuite · Poljana Rudera Boškovića · Od Margarite · M PERIĆA IZA GRADA · Vrata od Buže · Peline · Žudioska · PRIJEKO · Sinagoga · Od Puča · PLACA (STRADUN) · Luža · Tvrđava Minčeta · IZA GRADA · Peline · Palmotićeva · ŠIROKA · Od Puča · Dom Marina Držića · Isusovačka · Sv. Roka · Od Domina · Od Rupa · Etnografski Muzej Rupe · Od Kaštela · Samostan Sv. Marije · Danče · Sv. Spasa · Vrata od Pile · Pile · Od sorte

0 100 metres / 0 100 yards

The Onofrio Fountain, just inside Pile Gate

5–6

Turn right beside the statue to emerge on Pred Dvorom in front of the Rector's Palace (Knežev Dvor) with the cathedral to your right, then turn left to reach Luža, the broad square which marks the east end of Stradun. Above you is the 15th-century clock tower, heavily rebuilt, with a digital clock added in the early 21st century. Peer up to the top of the belfry and you may just be able to make out Maro and Baro, reconstructions of the original bronze figures who strike the hours with their hammers. Beneath the tower is a small fountain designed by Onofrio della Cava (➤ 175). In the middle of the square is another Dubrovnik landmark, the statue of an armoured knight at the foot of the Orlando Column. This remarkably gentle-looking figure is based on the cult of Orlando, the local name for the hero of the French epic poem *Chanson de Roland*. The original Roland was killed in battle in the Pyrenees, but the legend has been reinvented and has him ambushed by Saracens while defending Dubrovnik during the Crusades. During the time of the Ragusan republic, when Dubrovnik was an independent city-state, new laws were proclaimed from the Orlando Column and the statue's right arm was used as a unit of measurement (51.2cm/ 20 inches).

6–7

Turn left along Stradun and take the second right onto Ulica Žudioska. This was the main street of the 16th-century Jewish ghetto, whose gates were locked each night to keep the Jewish population in. A short way up on the left is the synagogue, which still serves a small Jewish community today and also contains an interesting museum (daily 10am–8pm, summer only).

At the top of the first flight of steps, you cross over Prijeko, the main thoroughfare of the upper town, running parallel to Stradun. Glance to your right to see the little Church of Sv. Nikola (St Nicholas) at the end of the street, with the remains of the Dominican monastery behind it. Continue climbing to the top of Ulica Žudioska to reach Peline.

7–8

Now you are in the highest part of town. Turn left along Peline, passing the Buža Gate (Vrata od Buže), one of five entrances to the

city. Take the right fork and continue along this street as it clings to the inside of the ramparts on its way to the Minčeta Tower (Tvrđava Minčeta), a two-floor circular fortress. The steep, narrow lanes to your left provide a series of wonderful vistas over the old town and back down to Stradun through a jumble of washing lines, balconies, staircases and potted plants. Turn left along Palmotićeva or any of the other streets to return to Stradun.

Taking a Break

There are numerous bars and cafés in the old town. For a drink with a view on a sunny day, you cannot beat Buža, reached through a gap in the city walls. A good spot for people-watching is the terrace of the Gradska Kavana, an old-style café between the clock tower and the Rector's Palace at Pred Dvorom 3. The restaurants along Prijeko are geared up for the tourist trade and mainly serve bland, overpriced food, but an exception is Rozarij (➤ 160).

The Stradun, which runs east–west through the city

5 Lokrum
Boat Trip/Walk

The wooded isle of Lokrum is Dubrovnik's summer garden, where people go to escape the city, to walk, swim and sunbathe, to breathe fresh air and indulge in romantic trysts. A day out on Lokrum makes a relaxing break from sightseeing in Dubrovnik – you can walk around the island in under two hours, but it is best to allow half a day, or bring your towel and swimwear (optional) and make a complete day of it.

The Boat Trip

Boats depart regularly in summer from the Old Harbour in Dubrovnik; check the time of the last boat back (it is usually 6pm). The trip across to the island takes about 15 minutes and the cost of the ticket includes admission to Lokrum.

DISTANCE 4km (2.5 miles) plus boat trip **TIME** 2–3 hours
START/END POINT Old Harbour, Dubrovnik ✚ 198 B1

The Walk

Step ashore at the harbour and climb the ramp beside the jetty. On your right is the old forest ranger's house, destroyed by Serbian shells in 1991 and now left abandoned as a memorial. From here, a well-signed network of walking trails leads across the island.

Take the footpath behind the house and stay on this shady lane as it clings to the northern shore, with occasional tracks through the trees leading to rocky beaches and bathing platforms. When the path forks, keep right above the shore, dropping down to reach the Cross of Triton, which commemorates the victims of a shipwreck in 1859.

Bear left above a small jetty and climb into the woods, leaving the shore behind. You soon reach Lazaret, the old quarantine hospital, enclosed by

The Lokrum Curse

Do not visit Lokrum if you are superstitious. Ever since the 19th century, there has been persistent talk of 'the curse of Lokrum', perhaps placed by Benedictine monks in revenge for the destruction of their monastery. One owner, Archduke Maximilian, became emperor of Mexico but was killed by his subjects in 1867; the island later passed to his nephew, Crown Prince Rudolf, who committed suicide in 1889. Today the island is uninhabited and there are few people who would be willing to spend the night there.

high walls designed to prevent infections from spreading. Take the path to the right around Lazaret and continue climbing until you come to the highest point of the island, crowned by a ruined French fortress, Fort Royal, dating from 1806. You can walk inside the star-shaped fort and climb the spiral staircase to the roof for 360-degree views of Dubrovnik, the whole of the sea as far south as Cavtat (▶157).

Leaving Fort Royal, take the path through the trees directly opposite where you entered

around to the right to reach the former Benedictine monastery. Although much of the building is off limits, you can wander around the dilapidated cloisters, which lead to an ornamental garden with a belvedere looking out to sea. Beyond the monastery, a path heads down to a swimming and sunbathing area. Instead, take the path signposted No. 4

Boats cross to Lokrum from Dubrovnik regularly

and drop down towards the middle of the island along the Rajski Put (Celestial Way), a processional route lined with tall cypress trees. Reaching a junction, turn right through the pine woods and go down the steps beside

a large reservoir, passing around the edge of a botanical garden. Turn left at the corner to walk through a beautiful wild olive grove with glimpses of the sea to your right. The botanical gardens are on your left, with numerous varieties of cactus and palm trees and peacocks strutting around. Follow the path

View across Lokrum from the French fort

to Mrtvo More (Dead Sea). Passing a children's playground, you reach this salt-water lake, connected to the sea by an underground channel. The water is shallow, so safe for children and non-swimmers.

Turn left on path No. 5 to return to the monastery on a woodland path, arriving in the landscaped Maximilian Gardens, from where it is a short stroll back to the harbour. Alternatively, for a longer walk, a series of footpaths leads around the wilder southern shore of the island, dropping down to Lokrum's popular naturist beach, with its concrete bathing platforms and dreamy views across the water to Cavtat.

Taking a Break

There is a restaurant inside the monastery cloisters, which is open in high summer. At other times, a small bar near the harbour (daily 9–6) sells sandwiches and cold drinks. A pleasant alternative is to buy picnic food in Dubrovnik and take it across to the island.

GETTING ADVANCE INFORMATION

Websites

▯ Croatian National Tourist Board:
www.croatia.hr

▯ Croatia web portal:
www.hr

▯ Ministry of Foreign Affairs (for visa information): www.mvp.hr

▯ Jadrolinija (ferry routes and timetables):
www.jadrolinija.hr

In the UK
Croatian National Tourist Office
2 The Lanchesters
162–164 Fulham Palace Road, London W6 9ER
☎ 020 8563 7979

BEFORE YOU GO

WHAT YOU NEED

● Required
○ Suggested
▲ Not required
△ Not applicable

Some countries require a passport to remain valid for a minimum period (usually at least six months) beyond the date of entry – contact their consulate or embassy or your travel agent for details.

	UK	Germany	USA	Canada	Australia	Ireland	New Zealand	France
Passport/National Identity Card	●	●	●	●	●	●	●	●
Visa (regulations can change – check before booking your trip)	▲	▲	▲	▲	▲	▲	▲	▲
Onward or Return Ticket	○	○	○	○	○	○	○	○
Health Inoculations (tetanus and polio)	▲	▲	▲	▲	▲	▲	▲	▲
Health Documentation	▲	▲	▲	▲	▲	▲	▲	▲
Travel Insurance	○	○	○	○	○	○	○	○
Driver's Licence (national)	●	●	●	●	●	●	●	●
Car Insurance Certificate	●	●	●	●	●	●	●	●
Car Registration Document	●	●	●	●	●	●	●	●

WHEN TO GO

Dubrovnik

High season   Low season

JAN	FEB	MAR	APR	MAY	JUN	JUL	AUG	SEP	OCT	NOV	DEC
11°C	12°C	14°C	17°C	21°C	25°C	28°C	28°C	25°C	21°C	16°C	13°C

☀ Sun   ☁ Cloud   🌧 Wet   🌦 Sun/Showers

The temperatures above are the average daily maximum for each month on the Adriatic islands and coast. Inland temperatures are considerably lower, often dropping below 0°C in Zagreb and highland areas in winter. Snow is common in the mountains. The sunniest place in Croatia is Hvar Town, which averages more than 2,700 hours of sunshine per year. During the summer months, the sea temperature can be as high as 28°C. The best months to visit are May, June, September and October, when there is less traffic and fewer tourists, but the sea is pleasantly mild. Late spring and early autumn are also good times for sailing and active holidays. The busiest months on the coast are July and August. Many hotels close down altogether between November and March.

In the US
Croatian National Tourist
Office
350 Fifth Avenue,
Suite 4003
New York, NY 10118
☎ 212/279-8672

In France
Croatian National Tourist
Office
Avenue Victor Hugo 48
75116 Paris
☎ 01 45 00 99 55

In Germany
Croatian National Tourist
Office
Kaiserstrasse 23
60311 Frankfurt
☎ 069 238 5350

GETTING THERE

By Air There are international airports at Zagreb, Split, Dubrovnik, Pula, Rijeka and Zadar. The national carrier, Croatia Airlines (www.croatiaairlines.hr), has regular flights to Zagreb from major European cities including London, Frankfurt, Paris and Rome. Links to North American cities are available through the Star Alliance network. Other airlines flying to Croatia include British Airways, Austrian Airways and Lufthansa. In summer, Croatia Airlines operates additional flights to the coastal airports and there are also numerous charter flights from British and European cities. Most seats on charter flights are sold by tour operators as part of a package holiday, but it is usually possible to buy a flight-only deal through travel agents or on the internet. Travellers to Istria can book no-frills flights with Ryanair to Trieste in Italy or Easyjet to Ljubljana in Slovenia.

By Sea Jadrolinija (www.jadrolinija.hr) operates car and passenger ferries between Italy and Croatia. The main routes are Ancona to Split and Bari to Dubrovnik, as well as the Adriatic coastal route linking Dubrovnik with Korčula, Stari Grad, Split, Zadar and Rijeka. Foot passengers can generally buy tickets at the quayside, but car passengers should book in advance. Ferries from Italy to Croatia are also operated by Sem Marina (www.sem-marina.hr), Adriatica (www.adriatica.it) and SNAV (www.snav.it). In summer, Adriatica also operates high-speed links from Trieste to Rovinj and the Brijuni Islands, while Venezia Lines (www.venezialines.com) has hydrofoils from Venice to Poreč, Pula and Rovinj.

By Land Croatia shares land borders with Slovenia, Hungary, Bosnia-Hercegovina and the Republic of Serbia and Montenegro. There are direct bus and rail links from Zagreb to most major European cities.

TIME

Croatia is on Central European Time, one hour ahead of Greenwich Mean Time. Summer time (GMT+2) operates from the last Sunday in March to the last Sunday in October.

CURRENCY AND FOREIGN EXCHANGE

Currency Croatia's currency is the kuna (kn), named after the pine-marten, whose fur was once used for trading. The kuna is divided into 100 lipa. Coins are issued in denominations of 1, 2, 5, 10, 20 and 50 lipa, 1kn, 2kn and 5kn. Notes are issued in denominations of 5, 10, 20, 50, 100, 200, 500 and 1,000kn. The euro (€) is widely accepted and many prices in tourist hotels are quoted in both euros and kuna.

Exchange Foreign currency and travellers' cheques can be changed at banks, travel agencies and hotels. You will need to show your passport when cashing travellers' cheques. You can also withdraw cash from ATM (cashpoint) machines in all towns and cities using your credit or debit card with a PIN (personal identification number). Your own bank will usually make a charge for this service.

Credit cards Major credit cards are widely accepted, though it is always advisable to have some cash.

TIME DIFFERENCES

GMT	Rome	USA New York	Germany	Croatia	Australia
12 noon	1 pm	← 7 am	→ 1 pm	→ 1 pm	→ Sydney 10 pm

WHEN YOU ARE THERE

CLOTHING SIZES

UK	Croatia/Europe	USA	
36	46	36	Suits
38	48	38	
40	50	40	
42	52	42	
44	54	44	
46	56	46	
7	41	8	Shoes
7.5	42	8.5	
8.5	43	9.5	
9.5	44	10.5	
10.5	45	11.5	
11	46	12	
14.5	37	14.5	Shirts
15	38	15	
15.5	39/40	15.5	
16	41	16	
16.5	42	16.5	
17	43	17	
8	34	6	Dresses
10	36	8	
12	38	10	
14	40	12	
16	42	14	
18	44	16	
4.5	38	6	Shoes
5	38	6.5	
5.5	39	7	
6	39	7.5	
6.5	40	8	
7	41	8.5	

NATIONAL HOLIDAYS

1 Jan	New Year's Day
Mar/Apr	Easter Monday
1 May	Labour Day
May/Jun	Corpus Christi
22 Jun	Anti-Fascist Resistance Day
25 Jun	Croatian National Day
5 Aug	Victory Day
15 Aug	Feast of the Assumption
8 Oct	Independence Day
1 Nov	All Saints' Day
25–26 Dec	Christmas

OPENING HOURS

○ Shops ● Offices ● Banks

● Post Offices ● Museums/Monuments ● Pharmacies

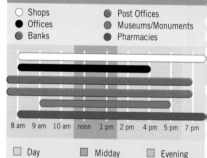

8 am   9 am   10 am   noon   1 pm   2 pm   4 pm   5 pm   7 pm

☐ Day   ■ Midday   ☐ Evening

Shops Most are closed on Saturday afternoon and all day Sunday. Some close for a break on weekday afternoons. Shopping centres in Zagreb, and shops in coastal resorts in summer, may stay open for longer hours and on Sundays.
Banks Generally open Mon–Fri 7–7, Sat 7–1.
Museums Opening hours vary widely, and it's best to consult the individual listings in this book. Many are closed on Mondays and weekend afternoons.
Pharmacies In larger towns, there will usually be a duty pharmacy open at night and weekends.
Post offices Main post offices are open Mon–Fri 7–7, Sat 7–1. Post offices in larger towns and cities stay open till 10pm.

POLICE 92

FIRE 93

AMBULANCE 94

PERSONAL SAFETY

Violence against tourists is unusual. Theft from cars is the most common form of crime. To be safe:

- Do not leave valuables on the beach or poolside.
- Always lock valuables in hotel safety deposit boxes.
- Never leave anything inside your car. If you have to, lock it out of sight in the boot.
- Beware of pickpockets in crowded markets, and on buses and trams in Split, Dubrovnik and Zagreb.
- Avoid discussions of the recent war, especially in ethnic Serb areas close to the Bosnian and Serbian borders.

Police assistance:
☎ **92 from any phone**

TELEPHONES

There are public telephones in all main towns. Phonecards (telefonska kartica) can be bought from post offices, news kiosks and shops with the HT (Hrvatski Telekom) logo. Mobile phone coverage is almost universal; the main network operators are Cronet and VIP. Make sure your phone is switched to international roaming before you go. The international dialling code for Croatia is 385.

International Dialling Codes
Dial 00 followed by

UK:	44
USA /Canada:	1
Irish Republic:	353
Australia:	61
Germany:	49

POST

Stamps can be bought at post offices and news kiosks. Postboxes are yellow and marked HP. Letters to EU countries generally arrive within 5 to 10 days, and to the US within two weeks. For urgent mail, use internet cafés in the main towns and resorts.

ELECTRICITY

The power supply is 220 volts AC. Sockets take two-pronged round continental plugs. Visitors from the UK will need an adaptor and visitors from the USA will need a transformer for 100–120 volt devices.

TIPS/GRATUITIES

Tipping is not expected for all services and rates are generally lower than elsewhere.

Restaurants	10 per cent
Taxis	10 per cent
Tour guides	10–20kn
Porters	10kn
Chambermaids	10kn per night
Lavatory attendants	No

CONSULATES and EMBASSIES

UK
☎ 01 600 9100

USA
☎ 01 661 2200

Ireland
☎ 01 667 4455

Australia
☎ 01 489 1200

New Zealand
☎ 01 488 1200

HEALTH

Insurance Citizens of EU countries receive free emergency medical treatment on production of their passport under a reciprocal health care agreement. This covers essential hospital stays, but excludes some expenses such as the cost of prescribed medicines. Private medical insurance is still advised and is essential for all other visitors.

Dental Services Dental treatment has to be paid for by all visitors, but is usually covered by private medical insurance.

Sun The sun is intense on the Adriatic coast in summer and you can burn very quickly. Cover up with a high-factor sunscreen, wear a hat and drink plenty of water. Children are especially vulnerable and need to be protected, especially near the sea.

Drugs Prescription and non-prescription drugs and medicines are available from pharmacies (ljekarna). Outside normal hours, a notice on pharmacy doors gives the address of the nearest duty chemist. Take adequate supplies of any drugs you need regularly as they may not be available. Other items to consider include insect repellent, anti-diarrhoea pills and sea-sickness tablets if you are going to be using the ferries.

Safe Water Tap water is safe to drink. Bottled mineral water is widely available.

CONCESSIONS

Young People Children under 12 pay half-price on most buses, trains and ferries, while children under three go free. An international student identity card (ISIC) gives discounts at museums and on public transport.
Senior Citizens Travellers over 60 may be entitled to discounted admission at museums and reduced fares on public transport.

TRAVELLING WITH A DISABILITY

Croatia has made great strides in providing facilities for travellers with disabilities, following a war in which many Croatians were disabled, but many older buildings are still inaccessible and cobbled streets in Dubrovnik and Zagreb are a particular problem for wheelchairs. Most modern hotels are suitable for disabled visitors. Before booking a holiday, discuss your particular needs with your tour operator or hotel.

CHILDREN

Hotels and restaurants are generally very child-friendly, and many hotels and campsites have playgrounds and children's pools. Most beaches are rocky rather than sandy, so plastic sandals are a good idea.

TOILETS

Public toilets can be found at bus and train stations. They usually make a small charge.

CUSTOMS

The import of wildlife souvenirs from rare and endangered species may be illegal or require a special permit. Before buying, check your home country's customs regulations.

LANGUAGE

The official language of Croatia is Croatian (hrvatski). Until 1991, this was known as Serbo-Croat, but it is now recognized as a separate language. Unlike Serbian, which uses the Cyrillic script, Croatian uses the Latin alphabet, though otherwise many words are identical. Croatian is entirely phonetic, which means that every word is pronounced exactly as it is written. Additional letters used in Croatian are č (pronounced 'ch'), ć (almost the same), š (pronounced 'sh'), ž (pronounced like a 'j') and đ (pronouned 'dj'). The letter 'c' is pronounced 'ts'.

GENERAL

hi **bog**
hello/good day **dobar dan**
good morning **dobro jutro**
good evening **dobra večer**
goodbye **doviđenja**
how are you? **kako ste**
please **molim**
thank you **hvala**
excuse me **oprostite**
yes **da**
no **ne**
here you are **izvolite**
cheers! **živjeli!**
large **veliko**
small **malo**
cheap **jeftin**
expensive **skupo**
Croatia **hrvatska**
America **amerika**
England **engleska**
I don't understand **ne razumijem**
do you speak English? **govorite li engleski?**
open **otvoreno**
closed **zatvoreno**

excuse me **izvinite**
tourist office **turistički ured**
embassy **veleposlanstvo**
consulate **konzulami ured**
cathedral **katedrala**
church **crkva**
garden **vrt**
library **knjižnica**
doctor **liječnik/doktor**
dentist **zubar**
police **policija**
hospital **bolnica**
entrance **ulaz**
exit **izlaz**

ACCOMMODATION

hotel **hotel**
room **soba**
single room **jednokrevetna soba**
double room **dvokrevetna soba**
apartment **apartman**
bath **kupaona**
shower **tuš**
toilet **zahod**
balcony **balkon**
telephone **telefon**
television **televizor**
breakfast **doručak**
half-board **polupansion**
key **ključ**
reservation **rezervacija**
campsite **autokamp**

RESTAURANT

restaurant **restauracija**
inn **konoba**
café **kavana**
cake shop **slastičarnica**
breakfast **doručak**
lunch **ručak**
dinner **večeru**
menu **jelovnik**
wine list **vinska karta**
the bill **račun**

NUMBERS

0	**nula**	10	**deset**		
1	**jedan**	11	**jedanaest**		
2	**dva**	12	**dvanaest**		
3	**tri**	13	**trinaest**		
4	**četiri**	14	**četrnaest**		
5	**pet**	15	**petnaest**		
6	**šest**	16	**šestnaest**		
7	**sedam**	17	**sedamnaest**		
8	**osam**	18	**osamnaest**		
9	**devet**	19	**devetnaest**		

20	**dvadeset**	200	**dvjesto**
30	**trideset**	300	**tristo**
40	**četrdeset**	400	**četristo**
50	**pedeset**	500	**petsto**
60	**šezdeset**	600	**šeststo**
70	**sedamdeset**	700	**sedamsto**
80	**osamdeset**	800	**osamsto**
90	**devedeset**	900	**devetsto**
100	**sto**	1000	**tisuću**
101	**sto i jedan**		

TRANSPORT

bus **autobus**
tram **tramvaj**
train **vlak**
bus station **autobusni kolodvor**
train station **zeljeznički kolodvor**
airport **zračna luka**
port **luka**
ferry **trajekt**
ticket **karta**
timetable **vozni red**
arrival **dolazak**
departure **odlazak**
taxi **taksi**
petrol **benzin**

MONEY

bank **banka**
exchange **razmjena**
exchange rate **tečaj**
cashier **blagajnik**
money **novac**
cash **gotovina**
banknote **novčanice**
coin **kovani novac**
credit card **reditna karta**
travellers' cheque **travel čekove**
post office **pošta**
stamp **poštanske marka**
postcard **razglednica**
telephone card **telekarta**

SHOPPING

bakery **pekara**
bookshop **knjižara**
butchers **mesnica**
cake shop **slastičarna**
pharmacy **ljekarna**
market **tržnica**
travel agent **putnička agencija**

TIME

hour **sat**
minute **minuta**
week **tjedan**
day **dan**
today **danas**
tomorrow **sutra**
yesterday **jučer**

MENU READER

barbun red mullet
bijelo vino white wine
blitva Swiss chard
breskva peach
brudet fish stew
čaj tea
čaj sa limunom tea with lemon
čevapčići spicy meatballs
crni rižot black risotto
crno vino red wine
češnjak garlic
cipal grey mullet
dagnje mussels
divlja svinija wild boar
džem jam
fiš paprikaš spicy fish stew
gazirana mineralna voda sparkling mineral water
govedina beef

grah beans
grčka cheese
grgeč perch
gulaš goulash
jabuka apple
jaje (jaja) egg (eggs)
janjetina lamb
jastog lobster
juha soup
kajmak clotted sour cream
kava coffee
krastavac cucumber
kruh bread
krumpir potatoes
kruške pears
kulen spicy salami
kupus cabbage
lignje squid
limun lemon
losos salmon trout
lozovača brandy
luben bass
luk onion
marelica apricot
maslinovo ulje olive oil
meso meat

mješana salata mixed salad
musaka moussaka
naranča orange
negazarina mineralna voda still mineral water
njoki gnocchi
ocat vinegar
oštrige oysters
ovčetina mutton
palačinke pancakes
papar pepper
paprike green peppers
paški sir sheep's cheese
pašticada beef with dumplings
pastrva trout
piletina chicken
pomfrit chips
pršut smoked ham
ragu thick soup
rajčica tomato
rak crab

rakija spirit
ramsteak rump steak
riba fish
riža rice
roze vino rosé wine
sardina sardines
sarma stuffed cabbage or vine leaves
sir cheese
škampi crayfish
sladoled ice-cream
slan salt
špinat spinach
šunka ham
svinjetina pork
tartufi truffles
teletina veal
travarica spirit flavoured with herbs
tuna tuna
ulje oil
voće fruits
voda water
zelena lettuce
zelena salata green salad
zubatac bream

Atlas

 Varaždin

ZAGREB
200/201

194/195

Osijek

196/197

Đakovo

Karlovac

Rijeka

Pula

192/193

Zadar

Split

198/199

DUBROVNIK
202

To identify the regions, see the map on the inside of the front cover

Regional Maps

Major route
Motorway
National road
Regional road
International boundary
National park
City area

Featured place of interest
Place of interest
City / town
Airport

192/199

| 0 | | 20 km |
| 0 | | 10 miles |

City Plans

Main road / minor road
Railway
Place of interest

Important building
Park
i Information

200/201

| 0 | | 200 metres |
| 0 | | 200 yards |

202

| 0 | | 150 metres |
| 0 | | 150 yards |

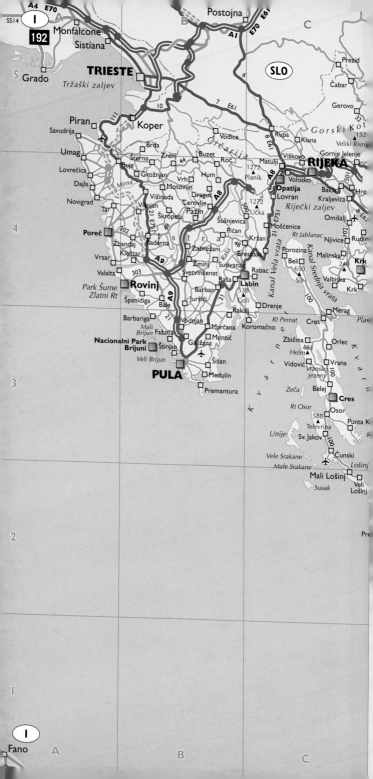

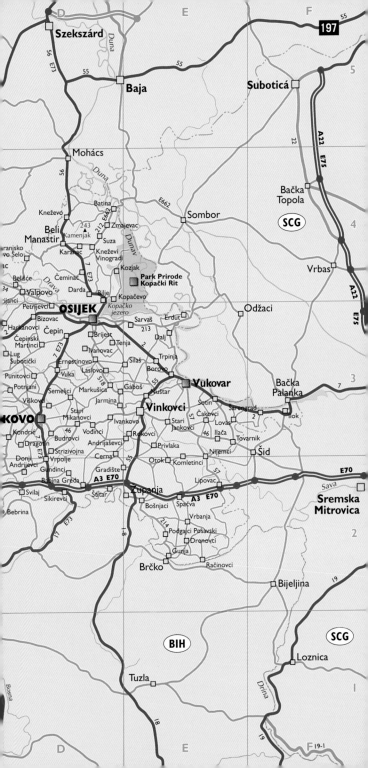

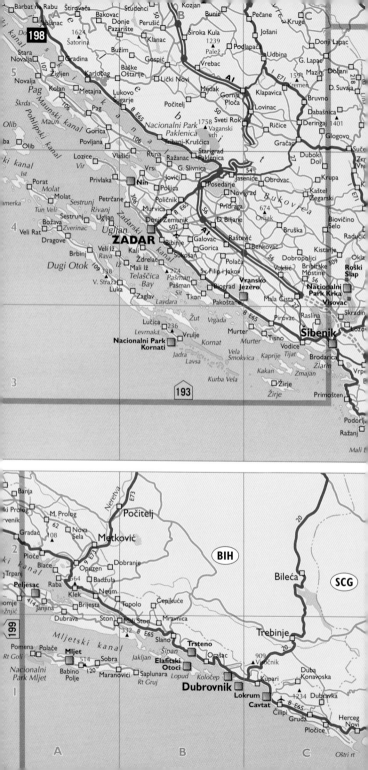

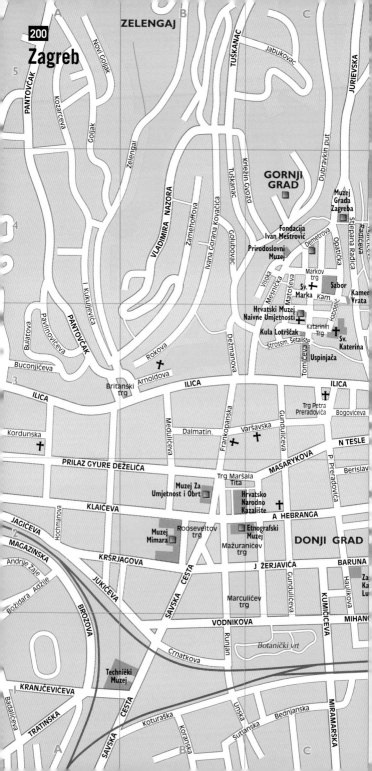

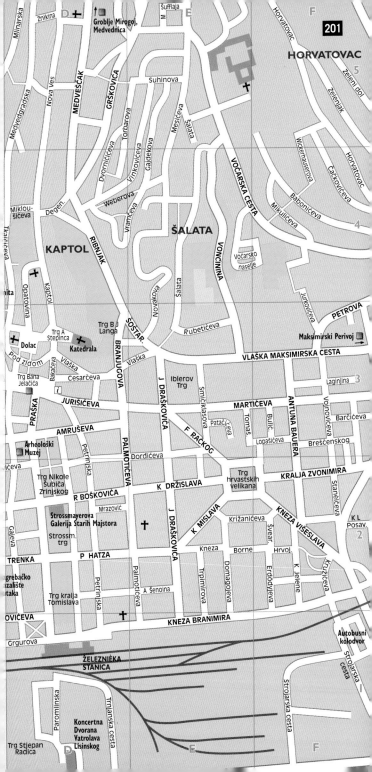

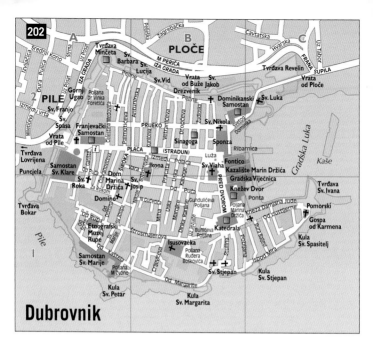

Dubrovnik

Picture credits

The Automobile Association wishes to thank the following photographers, libraries and associations for their assistance in the preparation of this book.

Abbreviations for terms appearing above: (t) top; (b) bottom; (l) left; (r) right; (c) centre (bg) background.

ADRIATICA.NET 26, 27; ALAMY 13 Chris Ballentine, 145t DIOMEDIA, 150 Nelly Boyd; CORBIS 8–9 Reuters, 23 Staffan Widstrand, 28 Susan Mullane/NewSport, 29 Paul Hanna/Reuters; CROATIAN NATIONAL TOURIST BOARD 14, 121, 151 Ivo Pervan, 99, 101l Milan Babic, 135tl Damir Fabijanic; REX FEATURES 100 SIPA; TOPFOTO 59 Françoise De Mulder/Roger–Viollet.
The remaining photographs are held in the Automobile Association's own photo library (AA PHOTO LIBRARY) and were taken by PETE BENNETT.

Questionnaire

Dear Traveller
Your comments, opinions and recommendations are very important to us. So please help us to improve our travel guides by taking a few minutes to complete this simple questionnaire.

You do not need a stamp (unless posted outside the UK). If you do not want to remove this page from your guide, then photocopy it or write your answers on a plain sheet of paper.

Send to: The Editor, Spiral Guides, AA World Travel Guides, FREEPOST SCE 4598, Basingstoke RG21 4GY.

Your recommendations...
We always encourage readers' recommendations for restaurants, night-life or shopping – if your recommendation is used in the next edition of the guide, we will send you a FREE AA Spiral Guide of your choice. Please state below the establishment name, location and your reasons for recommending it.

_____

_____

_____

_____

_____

Please send me AA Spiral _____
(see list of titles inside the back cover)

About this guide...
Which title did you buy?

_____ **AA Spiral**

Where did you buy it? _____

When? m m / y y

Why did you choose an AA Spiral Guide? _____

_____

_____

_____

Did this guide meet your expectations?

Exceeded ☐   Met all ☐   Met most ☐   Fell below ☐

Please give your reasons _____

_____

_____

_____

_____

continued on next page...

Were there any aspects of this guide that you particularly liked?

_____

_____

_____

_____

_____

Is there anything we could have done better?

_____

_____

_____

_____

About you...

Name (Mr/Mrs/Ms) _____

Address _____

_____

_____ Postcode _____

Daytime tel no _____ email _____

Please _only_ give us your email address and mobile phone number if you wish to hear from us about other products and services from the AA and partners by email or text or mms.

Which age group are you in?

Under 25 ☐   25–34 ☐   35–44 ☐   45–54 ☐   55–64 ☐   65+ ☐

How many trips do you make a year?

Less than one ☐   One ☐   Two ☐   Three or more ☐

Are you an AA member? Yes ☐   No ☐

About your trip...

When did you book? ⎕⎕/ y y   When did you travel? ⎕⎕/ y y

How long did you stay? _____

Was it for business or leisure? _____

Did you buy any other travel guides for your trip? ☐ Yes   ☐ No

If yes, which ones? _____

_____

Thank you for taking the time to complete this questionnaire. Please send it to us as soon as possible, and remember, you do not need a stamp (unless posted outside the UK).